A Time toWalk

Life Lessons Learned on the Appalachian Trail

Jay Platt

Eagle Eye Publishing

Carterville, Georgia

Printed in the United States of America
ISBN 0-9678938-0-1
SAN 253-1666

Published by Eagle Eye Publishing
38 River Birch Rd, Cartersville, GA 30121

Cover design by Linda Anderson
Cover photograph provided by the author
Produced with assistance from Griffith Publishing

TIME

*To everything
there is a season...*

*A time to be born,
and a time to die...*

*A time to kill,
and a time to heal...*

*A time to weep,
and a time to laugh...*

*A time to gain,
and a time to lose...*

*A time to love,
and a time to hate...*

—ECCLESIASTES 3:1-8

> *"On August 3, 1998, I set out on a journey of the Appalachian Trail. I guess it was my time to walk."*
>
> —Jay "Patch" Platt

CONTENTS

MY SINCEREST THANKS

Anyone who knows anything about success knows that the truly successful man doesn't become that way by himself. Show me someone who claims to be self made and I'll show you a fraud. I certainly realize that it's only through the help and guidance of many others that I've been able to accomplish the things I have in my life. In particular, I'd like to say:

To my loving wife, Paz. You are my support team, the one I can count on, and the reason I'm able to do the things I do. Thank you so much for being who you are, and for accepting me for who I am. I love you.

To my parents, Dawn and Joe. Thank you for always setting the proper example for me, and for all of your unconditional love and support.

To Maria "Bulldog" Shipton. Maria, you are one of a kind. Thank you for your friendship and for always going the extra mile.

To Joyce Graff, Peggy Marshall, and the rest of the VHLFA. Thank you for all that you do to help those of us affected by VHL.

To the United States Marine Corps. Thank you for instilling in me values that are all too uncommon our society today—like patriotism, integrity, commitment, and discipline.

To Earl Shaffer. Thank you for doing what the critics said was impossible, and allowing others to follow the trail you blazed.

Finally, and most importantly, to a loving God. Thank you for all of your many blessings, and for loving me enough to challenge me, develop me, and cause me to grow. Without you, *nothing* that I have today would be possible.

A LETTER TO THE READER

Dear Reader,

The book you're now reading actually had its beginnings in a conversation between my sister and me on January 23rd of 1999—the day I completed my southbound thru-hike of the Appalachian Trail.

My family, along with some friends from the Von Hippel Lindau Family Alliance, had come out in support of me on this, the final day of my over five-month hike from Maine to Georgia.

They'd met me for the final leg of my trek, a 0.9 mile walk to the top of Springer Mountain—something I had looked forward to for over 2,100 miles.

Once on top, I grabbed the trail register that was there, and since it was raining, took it to a nearby shelter to sign.

I'd thought a lot about what I might write in this final register, on my final day, on a trail that had affected me so profoundly over the past five months. But I was tired. Both physically and mentally. Actually, more like exhausted.

And so, with pen in hand, I wrote these poetic words. "Wahoo! I finished!" I then signed it, "Patch." That's it. That's all I wrote. I just didn't have the gumption to write more at the time. I hoped everyone would realize how tired I must be and would just let my lame entry go. But that wasn't to be the case.

My sister, Stacey, took one look at what I'd written, then shook her head and rolled her eyes, as only a big sister can do.

"Six months to contemplate the universe, and all you can write is, 'Wahoo! I finished!'" she said in exasperation.

In need of a response, I quickly replied, "Ah yes, but just wait for the book!"

Actually, I hadn't really thought about a book until that moment. But, as soon as I said what I did, it was as if divine intervention took over. From that day forward, I was a man with a new mission.

Once I decided to write it, I had some definite ideas about what I wanted to say, and how I wanted it said. Mainly, I didn't want it to be just another hiking book. There are plenty of those out there.

Rather, I wanted this book to be, not just about the Appalachian Trail, but about life itself. I hope by reading it, people will realize that I'm no big deal—anyone can do what I've done, if they'd just believe in themselves.

It shouldn't take you long to realize that authors like John Grisham, Tom Clancy, and Stephen King have nothing to fear from my writing abilities.

My writing style mirrors the way I strive to live my life—in a down-to-earth fashion. As you'll see, I've written in a simple and straightforward manner that I believe will make for easy reading. Of course, you'll ultimately be the judge of that.

For the purpose of keeping focused, I had to leave a good bit out of the book that I think you might find interesting. And now, thanks to the technological revolution, you don't have to miss any of it, because I've posted it all on my website at www.jayplatt.com.

There, you can read the journal I kept during my hike, which gives a true picture of my day-to-day life as a thru-hiker, or view some of my favorite photos from the trail, or find out what I consider to be my favorite moments of the trip. Plus a whole lot more....

I hope you'll look at this book as a starting point for your own journey. I believe if you read it with an open heart and mind, you'll walk away with a nugget or two, that you can use in your own life. But for now, read on, and I'll see you on the trail.

HAPPY TRAILS,
JAY "PATCH" PLATT

Ready to Go?

Meet Patch, Your Trail Guide

MEET PATCH, YOUR TRAIL GUIDE

I've learned there's something to be gained in all that we go through, especially the tough times.

—JAY "PATCH" PLATT

Wouldn't you agree that if you were about to take a trip into an unfamiliar wilderness, it would be a good idea to have a map, a compass, and a guide?

You'd probably want to know as much as possible about the area, and something about your guide's qualifications too. On that note, allow me to introduce myself and tell you a little about what to expect from this book.

3

My name is Jay "Patch" Platt, and in case you're wondering, "Patch" is my trail name. Most hikers use trail names to distinguish themselves more clearly than their real name would.

For instance, you might meet a lot of Johns or Steves on the trail, which could be hard to keep track of, but you probably wouldn't meet many hikers named "Patch."

Also, most trail names have some significance behind them, which tells you something about the hiker. The reason for my name is pretty obvious, considering that I wear a black patch over my left eye when I hike.

Unlike many authors of other so-called "self help" books out there, I'm not a psychologist, psychiatrist, or celebrity; and I'm not some New Age guru.

My professional background is that of a U.S. Marine, since that's basically all I've known my entire adult life.

I joined the Marine Corps straight out of high school in 1984, and loved every minute of it. After all, being a Marine was all I'd ever wanted to be since age eleven.

From day one, I planned on serving for twenty or more years, but I guess that wasn't meant to be.

Unfortunately, my career was cut short after fourteen years of service, because of my ongoing battle against a disease called Von Hippel Lindau syndrome (VHL). And a battle it's been! (See the appendix for more information on VHL.)

Since my initial diagnosis in 1986, I've come a long way, although having this disease has cost me a great deal over the years. Multiple operations (including the loss of my left eye), two failed marriages which were largely a result of all the stress the disease created, and the sudden ending of my Marine Corps career are just a few examples of the many struggles I've had to endure because of it.

Admittedly, at some points I've found living with it almost unbearable. But strangely enough, looking back, I have to say that having this disease has actually been a blessing of sorts.

Because of VHL, I believe I now see things much differently than I would otherwise. I've learned there's something to be gained in all that we go through, especially the tough times.

Although it's often difficult to see at first, if you look hard enough, it's there.

"What does not destroy me, makes me stronger."

—FREIDRICH NIETZSCHE

In 1998, my condition worsened and I was medically retired from the Marine Corps. This had a profound effect on me. After my retirement, I became more dedicated than ever to fighting the disease which had taken so much from me.

I was determined to prove that I wasn't "down for the count."

Although I was still recovering from back--to-back brain and kidney surgeries, I felt the need to do something to show both myself and the world that I wasn't going to let this disease beat me. But what could I do?

After looking at several options, I decided that hiking the entire Appalachian Trail (AT), known in hiker circles as a "thru-hike," was just the challenge I was looking for.

I did some research and found that of all the people who attempt the trail annually, about 98 percent hike from Georgia to Maine, or north-bound. Of the 3,000 hikers or so who begin the northbound trail each year, only about ten percent complete it.

---

*"All truly great thoughts are
conceived by walking."*

—FRIEDRICH NIETZSCHE

Though that in itself sounded challenging, I then found there had only been around 300 people who'd *ever* completed the trail going south, from Maine to Georgia.

Maybe it was the Marine in me, or maybe I'm just stubborn, but I decided to hike it as a southbounder.

I also wanted to do my part in raising money for cancer research. So I contacted the VHL Family Alliance (a nonprofit group dedicated to improving the treatment, quality of life and education of those affected by VHL) to tell them of my intentions.

I explained my goal was to raise $100,000 for their organization. I planned to ask for donations, or sponsors, like in a walkathon. The only difference was, I was going to be walking over 2,100 miles.

I think I shocked them when I explained my plan. But, nevertheless, they wished me good luck. They even developed a special section on their website, www.vhl.org, that was used to track my progress. As a result, hundreds of people were able to "virtually" follow me as I moved down the trail.

"If you can dream it, you can do it."

—WALT DISNEY

I began my hike atop Mt. Katahdin, Maine, on August 3, 1998. The trail turned out to be much harder than I'd anticipated. Although I'd been a Marine for over fourteen years and had trained all over the world, I found out that wasn't enough to prepare me for such an endeavor. Looking back, I'm not sure anything could. It's one of those things you've got to just do!

On January 23, 1999, more than five months and 2,160 miles later, I completed my trek atop Springer Mountain, Georgia. Even more importantly, after all was said and done, over $109,000 was raised as a result of my hike!

I learned a lot about life during my time on the AT. Some days were cold, wet and miserable. Others were filled with the kind of awe-inspiring scenery that I could never fully describe.

Through it all, I discovered what I believe are some valuable lessons about life. That's where this book comes in. It's a book that's for everyone, because it's about issues that relate to us all.

In every chapter, you will find practical ideas and principles—I call these life lessons—which will enable you to gain the success, happiness and satisfaction you want and deserve out of life.

Each lesson is illustrated through real life examples of my experiences which occurred during my time on the Appalachian Trail.

Here then, is a sample of what this book will do for you; it will teach you...

- Why life is like a mountain trail (page 15)

- The reason you should guard your thoughts very carefully (page 27)

- How to determine if you're a chicken or a pig (page 47)

- What I learned about attitude by surviving a hurricane on top of a mountain (page 59)

- Why you shouldn't judge a book by its cover (page 71)

- Why five minutes is more time than you think (page 85)

- The valuable lesson a rat taught me on overcoming fear (page 99)

- The reason you should live each day as if it's your last (page 113)

- Why you should count your blessings for all that you have (page 131)

- How to loosen yourself from limiting behaviors (page 143)

- And much more…

Well, you've now met your trail guide and have received a briefing on the area in which you'll be traveling. The next move is yours. When you're ready to go, turn the page and let the adventure begin.

SUCCESS

*"To laugh often and much,
to win the respect of intelligent
people and the affection of children,
to earn the appreciation of honest
critics and endure the betrayal of false
friends, to appreciate beauty, to find
the best in others, to leave the world a
bit better, whether by a healthy child,
a garden patch, or a redeemed social
condition; to know even one life has
breathed easier because you have
lived. This is to have succeeded!"*

—RALPH WALDO EMERSON

CONTROL YOUR ATTITUDE

*Hiking the
Trail of Life*

Hiking the Trail of Life

"Life is like hiking on a mountain trail..."

Have you ever studied the lives of the great philosophers, writers and thinkers? Men and women who have changed the course of history and made a real difference in the world. Jesus Christ, Abraham Lincoln, Martin Luther King, Jr., Ghandi, Mother Teresa, Norman Vincent Peale, Og Mandino... The list goes on and on.

It's amazing how powerful their words are and how much of an impact they make today even though they're no longer physically with us. You can learn a great deal from them all. But, I'd venture to say there is one man who you probably have not considered, even though he too has a lot of important things to say. His name is Forrest Gump.

Forrest, of course is a fictional character from the book and movie about his life. Forrest was full of sayings that, while on the surface were unusual, meant a lot. One of his most profound was, "Life is like a box of chocolates; you never know what you're gonna get."

The reason this and his other statements were so powerful is that what he said was so true. There's even a name for his words of wisdom; they're called "Gumpisms."

While I don't claim to be in the same class as Forrest Gump or any other philosopher, I'd like to try my hand here at a "Patchism:" *"Life is like hiking on a mountain trail; it's level at times, but it's mixed with hard climbs up and easy climbs down."*

I came up with that philosophy during my time on the AT, and I believe, as with the Gump sayings, it holds truth for everyone. It applies no matter what your background, race or gender may be because, the fact of the matter is, we've all got our own trail to hike, the trail of life.

It wasn't long after the start of my thru-hike that I began to see the comparison between hiking and life itself. Each day of my hike was reminiscent of a mini lifetime, full of surprises. To paraphrase Forrest, you never knew what you were going to get.

Some times were up, some were down, some were filled with breathtaking scenery, and some were downright miserable. Just like what we experience over the course of a lifetime.

"If we had no winter, the spring would not be so pleasant; if we did not sometimes taste of adversity, prosperity would not be so welcome."

—ANNE BRADSTREET

I learned on the trail, as in life, there are three stages that you pass through as you continue along your path. I call these the level, climbing and downhill stages.

An important point to remember here is that usually there is no way of knowing when we'll pass through a particular stage. Therefore, we must be prepared for any and all of them. Let's take a closer look at each stage as it applies to our life.

First, we'll discuss the level stage of our "hike." This is where most of us spend the majority of our lives. In this stage, nothing's going on that's really that great, but nothing's that bad either. It's our comfort zone.

From that description, this must be a good stage to be in, right? While on the surface, it's certainly better than the hard times, there are several potential problems which can result for those who never venture away from this stage.

One problem is complacency. People tend to settle into their comfort zone and then are unwilling to leave it, even though things could be better with just a little more effort.

This type of thinking reminds me of a story about a dog that was lying on a nail and whimpering. Someone asked the dog's owner why it didn't just move off the nail, when that's all it would take to stop the pain. The owner replied, "I guess it just doesn't hurt bad enough yet."

That's how it is with a lot of people. Even though things could be better if they'd just get off the "nail," they stay and try to make it as comfortable as possible. They've traded a great life for a fair one and so never live up to their full potential. Then they look back on their life and say, I sure wish I'd...

I met a guy on the trail—named Trail Buzzard—who was like that. He was a great guy and all, but he was just unwilling to get out of his comfort zone. To complete such a hike requires that you do just that.

You can't walk over 2,100 miles by only going four or five miles a day and expect to finish in a reasonable amount of time. Trail Buzzard had begun his thru-hike over two months before me, yet I and many others caught and later passed him.

His problem was that although he talked like he wanted to complete the trail, his actions never lined up with his words. The last time I saw him was in Pennsylvania. I was later told that he'd gotten off the trail and had gone home.

As a thru-hiker, I can tell you that although it's easier to only do a few miles each day, it's not the way to complete the hike. You've got to be willing to go the extra mile.

Another potential problem in this stage, is a lack of preparedness for the hard times that are bound to come. Many people who fall into this trap don't know how to handle stressful situations because, quite frankly, they've never extended themselves.

Because of this, they treat mole hills like mountains. Or as the popular phrase goes, they "sweat the small stuff." People like this are constantly involved with some "tragedy" in their life. When you ask them how they're doing, you get a full listing of how bad things are for them, etc. Then, when they're faced with a real challenge they're unable to handle it.

So what should you do if you find yourself in this stage? Venture out. Try something new. Push yourself. Only by challenging yourself during this stage, will you be prepared for the next stage we'll discuss, the toughest stage, the stage when we must climb the mountain.

"Most of our obstacles would melt away if, instead of cowering before them, we would make up our minds to walk boldly through them."

—ORISON SWETT MARDEN

Imagine you're standing at the base of a 6,000-ft mountain, with a sixty-pound pack on your back. As you stare up at it, in awe of its magnitude, you wonder to yourself, "How in the world am I ever gonna make it up something that big?"

Eventually, you somehow talk yourself into giving it a try. Within minutes of beginning to climb, your legs feel like rubbery noodles under the weight of the pack. They're screaming for a break. Your chest feels like an elephant is sitting flat in its center, and you're certain your lungs are being squeezed to the bursting point. You fully expect your heart to literally explode at any moment. All the while you're thinking to yourself, "It can't possibly get any harder than this, can it? Is this ever going to end? I'm not sure I can keep going." But as long as you keep placing one foot in front of the other, you'll continue to move up that mountain. Little by little, step by step.

I found myself in that exact situation many times during my thru-hike. One day that really stands out in my mind was my first on the trail. It was the day I climbed the much talked about Mount Katahdin.

Katahdin is a tough climb, let me tell you. There are places that you have to pull yourself up and over rocks, and then walk along ledges where on either side there are drop-offs of one thousand plus feet. One false step and you'd be over the edge. It was my first taste of such a mountain, and it was much harder than I expected.

But I made it. And I continued to make it up and over every other mountain I came to, all the way to Georgia. Not because I'm something special, but because I refused to quit just because it was hard at times. There's a valuable lesson in that for all of us, as we live our daily lives.

One common denominator we all share in this world is the assurance that if we stick around long enough, we'll eventually have to face hard times. These hard times can come in various ways.

Maybe it's by suffering the loss of a loved one through death or divorce; or it could be your getting diagnosed with cancer or an equally devastating disease—or a multitude of other tragedies that explode into people's lives.

The point is this: I don't know of anyone who's immune to difficult times. If you haven't had yours yet, be ready, because chances are you will. I don't tell you this to scare you, but rather to prepare you. By arming yourself now, you'll be prepared for when the hard times do come.

These tough times represent the difficult, "climbing" stage of our "hike." They test our mettle and ultimately strengthen us. And just like climbing a mountain, the most important thing is to not quit. Just keep plugging away at it, clawing every inch of the way if necessary. You can rest assured that if you continue to move forward, eventually you'll get to the top, which leads to an easier downhill grade.

This brings us to the third and final stage that we'll discuss—the downhill. These are the times in our lives when everything seems to be going perfectly, those times when it seems as if we can do no wrong.

Maybe we've just fallen in love, or have gotten a big job promotion, or maybe straight A's in school. These times are great. By all means, enjoy them! It's the same feeling you get when you're cruising down a smooth trail coming off a mountain. You're able to catch your breath and look around. You feel great. During these times, it's easy to forget how hard it was to reach the top.

During the first half of my hike, after struggling to get to the top of a mountain, I'd just about run down the other side. Finally, after many falls and a twisted knee and ankle, I learned my lesson.

One day in particular woke me up to the danger of this. It was the day I almost fell off the side of a mountain in Maine.

I was coming down a steep decline, moving quicker than I should have. Then, without warning, I tripped and fell headfirst! As I was falling, I was able to roll in such a way that changed the position of my head and feet. Although now going feet first, I was nevertheless still sliding. As I looked down at my feet, I could see that I was fast approaching a 1,000-ft drop-off!

Somehow, just before sailing over the edge, my right foot caught a root. I was sliding with such force from the weight of the pack that my right leg was ripped backward placing my foot behind me. Although painful, it was definitely better than what was awaiting me a few yards away.

This, along with several other tumbles, taught me the value of enjoying the downhill and not rushing through it.

More than that, I came to realize that another hard climb waited just ahead—it was just a matter of time. I didn't dread the climb; I was just prepared for it. And the same should apply to our lives.

Sadly, far too many people don't understand this concept. They live as if their current situation will never end. Of course, that simply isn't the case.

While the saying, "nothing lasts forever" may not be true in all situations, it certainly is here. It's imperative that you understand that neither good times nor bad will last forever. And there really isn't much you can do about it.

The fact that hard times are inevitable doesn't mean that you have to be miserable. On the AT, I never would have gotten to see all the great views I did if it weren't for the climbing. Although I often cursed the mountain at the time, I was always proud of what I'd accomplished when I stuck it out and made it to the top. The view from there made it all worthwhile. And I knew that in the process I was becoming a better person along the way.

"The last of the human freedoms
is to choose one's attitudes."

—VICTOR FRANKL

The same goes with all of the hard times I've faced in my life. I'm not saying that if given the opportunity to not go through some of the struggles I've faced I would, but I do believe that because of them I've grown into a much better person than I'd be without having gone through them.

The bottom line is this: Ultimately, how you handle life's ups and downs comes down to your attitude. If you get knocked down, you can stay there, or you can get back up. You can continue to try, or you can quit and cry. You can whine, or you can shine. It's all up to you. Like Shakespeare said, "There is nothing either good or bad, but thinking that makes it so."

It really is a matter of perspective. You can find happiness and joy no matter where you are on your "hike." This is what Abraham Lincoln, a man who had a lot of pain in his life, said about happiness: "A man is about as happy as he makes up his mind to be." That really says it all. So make up your mind to be happy, no matter where you are on the trail.

ATTITUDE

"The longer I live, the more I realize the impact of attitude on life. Attitude, to me, is more important than facts. It is more important than the past, than education, than money, or circumstances, than failures, than successes, than what other people think, say, or do.

It is more important than appearance, giftedness, or skill. It will make or break a company, a church, a home. The remarkable thing is, we have a choice every day regarding the attitude we will embrace for that day.

We can not change our past. We can not change the fact that people will act in a certain way. We can not change the inevitable. The only thing we can do is play on the one string we have, and that is our attitude. I am convinced that life is 10% what happens to me and 90% how I react to it. And so it is with you. We are in charge of our attitudes."

—REVEREND CHARLES SWINDOLL

LESSON TWO

THE POWER OF THE MIND

Ghost Story

GHOST STORY

*"You can never get away from
yourself. The outside world may
not hear what you say, but your
mind does. It's always there.
Waiting, listening, recording."*

—JAY "PATCH" PLATT

Do you believe in ghosts? Come on now, be honest. I'd venture to say that you, like me, at least believe in the possibility of their existence. But if you'd asked me that question prior to my thru-hike, I probably wouldn't have been so up front with you. I might have even said, "No way!" and told you that I thought people who believed in such nonsense were a little bit nutty. But that was before my run-in with a ghost!

It happened in Virginia. A hiker named Grunt and I were together at the time. I'd met Grunt the day before. He'd walked up on me while I was kicked back with my boots off, taking a much needed break and soaking up some sun. He seemed to appear from nowhere and really surprised me. You see, at that point, I'd been convinced for weeks that I was the only southbounder left on the trail. I really enjoyed his company.

Grunt had left Katahdin a couple of weeks after me and had been consistently doing twenty-plus mile days ever since. He said he'd been reading my register entries for quite awhile and had made it a goal to catch me. He'd recently split up with a couple of guys that he'd hiked with all the way from Katahdin, so I think he was probably looking to hook up with another hiking partner.

We hitched into town that day for some grub and then walked a few miles out to the next shelter. That night was as normal as the rest had been during my trip, but little did I know what was waiting up the trail!

The next morning we took off at daybreak with a plan of doing fifteen miles to the next shelter. The terrain in that area was extremely tough and mountainous. After an exhausting day of hiking, we pulled into Punchbowl shelter around 5 p.m. or so.

As the sun began to set for the evening, we busied ourselves with cooking our dinner, getting water, etc. As I was waiting for some water to boil, I grabbed the register and looked it over. As I read it, one of the entries caught my attention.

"People only see what they are prepared to see."

—RALPH WALDO EMERSON

Someone had written, "If you see or hear anything strange in these woods, please contact me." It went on, "If you do see or hear something, you'll know exactly what I mean." There was an address listed.

There were also some other entries from hikers who gave dire warnings about staying at this shelter. Now I ask you, what would you think after reading something like that?

I just sort of laughed it off and gave the register to Grunt to read. We both agreed that it was just an example of someone trying to play with our heads. But inside, I began to wonder.

We ate dinner and then went to bed around seven. All was normal until midnight. I'd fallen asleep fairly quickly that night, but didn't sleep very soundly. I could tell that Grunt was sleeping about as well me by the way he was tossing and turning on the other side of the shelter.

About 11:30, I got up for my nightly call of nature. I slipped on my boots, then stepped outside. I immediately noticed that the area surrounding the shelter was shrouded in a thick fog. The small pond, about a hundred feet away, could barely be made out in the light of the full moon shining above. The fog seemed to have rolled in from nowhere, as it had been a clear night when we went to bed. The normally silent night was now filled with the chatter of bullfrogs: "Ribbut, Ribbut, Ribbut."

After returning to the shelter, I lay back down but couldn't get back to sleep. I kept thinking over and over again about what I'd read earlier in the register. What did it mean? Could there be something to it?

As my mind began to race, I couldn't help but think about all the horror movies I'd seen over the years. Movies like "Halloween," "Friday the Thirteenth," and "The Exorcist." But those were just movies, right?

As I tried to convince myself there was nothing to be afraid of, I thought I heard the sound of footsteps coming toward the shelter. The sound was so faint, though, that I could barely make it out.

Straining my ears to make out the noise, I became convinced that someone was, ever so slowly, approaching the shelter; as if they were trying to sneak up on us! That's right, someone, not something. After being in the woods for as long as I'd been at that point, I'd gotten pretty good at identifying the difference in sound between people and animals walking. This definitely didn't sound like an animal.

The sound continued, only now closer to the shelter. At this point, my heart was beating so loudly that it made it difficult to make out the noise. Then it disappeared. Where had it gone? Without warning, it appeared again, this time in front of the shelter. Then the side, then the rear.

The wind picked up and the leaves began to rustle all around, but if you listened closely enough, you could make out what sounded like a faint whisper saying, "Come outside." Was I scared? You better believe it!

Finally, with a sense of dread, I forced myself to get up and take a look. When I did, from the sound of it, whatever was there ran away, although I must admit that I never actually caught sight of anything.

As you might guess, I didn't sleep much the rest of that night. The next morning, at first light, Grunt and I got our gear together and hiked out of there as quickly as possible.

After an hour or so, as we crossed the top of Bluff Mountain, we came upon a memorial that was covered in rabbit's feet, coins, tokens, etc. I suppose people had left them as a sign of respect. The memorial was for a little girl named Ottie who had gone missing in that area in the late 1800's. She'd apparently wandered away during a family outing and was never seen alive again.

Grunt and I just sort of looked at each other as if to say, "Are you thinking what I'm thinking?" We then each confessed how scared we'd been the night before.

This story really makes you think, doesn't it? To this day, I'm not exactly sure of what I experienced that night. Whether something was really there or not, I don't know. But one thing's for sure, that night I fell victim to the power of the mind.

It's been proven that our subconscious mind doesn't differentiate between what's real and what's not. For that reason, we must be very careful about what we expose ourselves to. You never know how it will affect you later.

Looking back on that night I realize a couple of things. First of all, when I read the register entries that hinted of strange happenings in the area, I was unknowingly being coaxed into believing that something would happen that night. Also, my copy of *The Thru-Hikers Handbook* told of a rumor of a ghost in that area. If you add to that, my years of being conditioned by watching various horror movies, it becomes more clear how I experienced what I did.

"Watch your thoughts, they become your words. Watch your words, they become your actions. Watch your actions, they become your habits. Watch your habits, they become your character. Watch your character, for it becomes your destiny."

—UNKNOWN

My experience was no different than the way a "witch doctor" is able to put a "death curse" on someone, and then that person dies.

The "witch doctor" has no real power over the "cursed" person, other than the power to make him believe that he did.

So how does all of this apply to you? Let's first look generally, then we'll get down to specifics.

Most of us are influenced by outside forces almost everyday, in one form or another; usually without our knowledge or understanding. It's the reason we act, talk, and do the things we do.

Advertisers learned a long time ago that they could steer our buying habits by exposing us to the right types of messages. They could literally condition us.

If you doubt that's true, then try to answer the following questions: What drink is the real thing? What is less filling and tastes great? What's good to the last drop? What's the drink of the new generation? If you answered any of those correctly, then you've been conditioned.

This conditioning is well illustrated in the following story: A mother was quizzing her three-year old son on animal sounds. "What sound does a dog make?" she asked. "Ruff, Ruff," the boy replied. "Good," the mother praised.

"What about a cat?" she went on. "Meow," the boy correctly answered. "Very good" the mother said.

"And what about a frog?" Without hesitation, he replied, "Bud."

I hope by now I've convinced you of how powerful the mind really is. How you use its power is up to you. You can use it to help you become more healthy, wealthy and wise. Or, as so many others, you can literally program it for failure. Let's take a closer look.

Imagine your mind as a computer. Not just any computer though, a super computer. A computer so powerful, there's nothing that man could ever build to compare with its virtually unlimited capacity. A capacity so astounding that it's been estimated that the average person only uses three to four percent of it.

Although this computer is empty when you first get it (when you're born), it quickly begins filling its database. The truly amazing thing about this computer is the way it records its data. Unlike your desktop PC, this computer records everything it comes into contact with, automatically. This means that it not only records during those times when you are intentionally inputting information, but also during the times when you are totally unaware.

So what does this mean? It means that you, as the programmer, need to exert as much control as possible over your "computer." Here's how.

Let's begin with the question of, what do you read? Or do you even read at all? Are you reading uplifting and inspiring books that can change you for the better? Or are you wasting your by mind by reading trashy novels and magazines? Do you take your advice on life from the likes of Solomon and Plato, or the *National Enquirer* and *Cosmo*?

Books have the power to touch your soul. The right book can change your life for the better. The libraries are full of them. But chances are, you won't even have to leave your house to find the greatest success book ever written. It's possibly tucked away somewhere in your home right now, collecting dust. It's full of so many powerful principles on how to live your life, that it's known as the **B**asic **I**nstructions **B**efore **L**eaving **E**arth. I suggest you find it and read what it has to say.

The next question is, what do you watch on television or at the movies? Doesn't it make sense that what you fill your mind with, by watching a TV program or movie, will have a later effect on you? It certainly did on me when I was in the woods all alone, especially the night I encountered Little Ottie. Rest assured, what you watch does have a profound effect on your mind. If a show like Jerry Springer is your idea of good family entertainment, you aren't exactly preparing yourself to win friends and influence people.

Finally, what do you say to yourself? This probably has more impact on your success or failure than any other one thing. Literally, what you say is what you get. Remember, you can never get away from yourself. The outside world may not hear what you say, but your mind does. It's always there. Waiting, listening, recording.

When you say things like "I can't," or "I'm nothing but a loser," it hears you and takes action to ensure your commands are carried out.

Conversely, having a *can-do* attitude will do wonders for you. You'd be able to do far more than you ever thought you could if you'd only believe in yourself. Henry Ford understood this when he said, "If you think you can or think you can't, you're right."

We're also affected greatly by what others say to us, just as we affect others by what we say. That's why we should all be mindful about the words we use, particularly to children, who have very impressionable minds.

Words have the power to build or destroy. As the little boy in the example thought frogs said, "Bud," after watching the Budweiser Frogs commercials, so will a child come to believe that he or she is stupid, worthless, or unwanted if told so enough times.

Although there are many other factors involved, it basically all comes down to this: Your mind belongs to you. It's like a fertile field and you're the farmer. If you're planting weeds, then don't expect corn to come up. As I heard a wise man once say, crap seeds produce a crap crop. So what are you planting?

BELIEVE IN YOURSELF

"You are your greatest asset,
there is nothing you can't do.
No one can keep you from dreaming,
only you can stop them coming true.
Your achievements are determined
by the desire that you possess.
Believe in who you are.
Believe in what you do.
It's not a quirk of fate
It's strictly up to you."

—UNKNOWN

LESSON THREE

COMMIT YOURSELF

Which Are You?

WHICH ARE YOU?

---

*"Too often we look at someone
who has achieved greatness in
some area of their life with envy.
But what we fail to take into
account, is the amount of
commitment it took for them to
reach that point."*

—JAY "PATCH" PLATT

A re you a chicken or a pig? I realize most people are probably confused by such a question, and a few may even be offended. But by the time you're finished with this lesson, you'll understand why I asked.

Before I explain this question any further, though, let me first ask you another. What is that you want out of life, and what are you willing to do to attain it?

I believe this question is vitally important because I'm a firm believer that you can accomplish virtually anything you set your mind to. However, if you truly want to succeed, it's gonna take more than just *wanting* it to happen.

It's gonna take more than a half-hearted attempt, with a plan to quit as soon as things get tough, and it'll take more than simple involvement.

The truth is, more often than not, it requires a decision that come hell or high water, you won't quit until you have accomplished your goal. In a word, it takes *commitment*.

What exactly is commitment, anyway? Webster's dictionary defines it as something pledged, an agreement or pledge to do something, or the state or an instance of being obligated or emotionally impelled.

While those are good book definitions, they unfortunately don't provide a concrete example of the difference between true commitment and simple involvement—which brings me back to my original question. Are you a chicken or a pig?

Each morning all across America, people sit down at the breakfast table for a hearty plate of ham and eggs. It's doubtful, however, they realize the valuable lesson that can be learned from the meal they're about to eat.

It's a lesson that explains why some people succeed against the odds, while others flounder, why some people achieve greatness, and others mere mediocrity. It explains all of this and more.

You see, in order for the breakfast to be prepared, both the chicken and the pig had to give something up. The difference is in how much they gave.

To produce the eggs, the hen had to lay them. Therefore, she was *involved* in the process of delivering them. But the pig, he was *committed*. In order to make the ham, he gave it everything he had!

I've always considered that to be a great example of what true commitment is all about. Unfortunately, the truth is, there are far more chickens in this world than pigs.

Too often we look at someone who has achieved greatness in some area, such as a star athlete or musician, with envy. We think to ourselves how much we'd love to be in their shoes.

They seem to have it all. They make what they do look so easy.

"The quality of a person's life is in direct proportion to their commitment to excellence, regardless of their chosen field of endeavor."

—VINCE LOMBARDI

But what we fail to take into account, is the amount of commitment it took for them to reach that point. All the hours and hours of practice, the early morning workouts, etc. In other words, the commitment level of the pig.

As I was to learn, thru-hiking certainly falls into the category of an endeavor that requires pig-like commitment. Without total commitment to finishing, chances are you won't.

During my time on the trail, I saw plenty of people go home early. Some gave up after only a few days, some it took weeks, and some lasted months. They all walked away, however, without finishing what they'd set out to.

Even though I'm sure they wanted to complete the trail, they were missing that vital ingredient of being totally committed. That's not to say they were bad people. They were just unwilling to commit the time and energy required.

Thru-hikers hike for reasons as diverse as the hikers themselves. In my case, I guess I had something to prove, not really to others, but to myself.

My release from the Marine Corps had hit me pretty hard. In a matter of a year's time, I'd gone from being a Physical Training Instructor to being medically retired after being found unfit for further service.

Although on the outside I took it well enough, on the inside, where it counts, I was in turmoil. I felt like I'd somehow failed and I needed to prove to myself that I could make a comeback.

Initially, I thought of running from one coast to the other. I figured it would take at least six months to get from North Carolina to California. I got the idea from a Canadian that I'd read about, by the name of Terry Fox.

Terry, after losing his left leg to cancer, attempted to run across Canada to raise money for cancer research. Sadly, he died before he was able to complete the run. His example inspired me, as I'm sure it has many others. He definitely had the commitment level of the pig. He died in the pursuit of an awesome goal.

After researching the viability of doing such a run myself, however, I decided it wasn't in the cards for me. Logistically, it was just too difficult to pull off. There had to be something else.

That's when I happened upon the idea of hiking the Appalachian Trail. After several days of research, I made the decision to do it. Once my decision was made, I then started telling everyone I knew about my plan. That, by the way, is a valuable tip which shouldn't be overlooked.

---

*"Those who say it can't be
done are being passed by
those doing it."*

—UNKNOWN

By telling others what I was going to do, I was intentionally putting my back against the wall and making it difficult on myself to quit. This works because no one likes to fail, especially in front of others. This technique of putting your back against the wall can be helpful in virtually any goal you set for yourself. It does wonders to help keep you committed when the going gets tough.

The next thing I did was contact the VHL Family Alliance. I explained my goal of raising money for cancer research, by hiking the AT. I knew that as soon as others began to donate money, I simply *had* to finish. In other words, I cut off my avenues of retreat. Or, as the following story illustrates, I burned my ships in the harbor.

A General landed on an island with three hundred soldiers. Their mission was to seize the beach and hold it until reinforcements arrived the next day. The enemy was known to be a fierce and ruthless adversary who'd never lost a battle.

As the soldiers were disembarking from their ships, he overheard some of them saying to one another that if the going got too tough, they'd simply retreat to the ships and sail away. Upon hearing this, the General ordered that the ships be burned in the harbor. His men, with nowhere to retreat, won the battle and held the area.

Unfortunately, most people are simply unwilling to "burn their ships." They, like the General's men, want them there, just in case things get too hard. That way they can use them to escape with. But that's not the way of true commitment.

No. If you really want to be committed, then you must decide now to follow the General's example, and burn your ships in the harbor. You must decide to be less like the chicken, and more like the pig. Because I'm a firm believer that, although they might not describe it in the same manner as I have, all people who've made a mark in this world have been willing to commit themselves this way.

Consider people like the young musician who moves to Nashville against the advice of his friends and family, or the actor who goes to Hollywood in hopes of landing a big movie role, or the business person who risks his or her life savings to fund their business start-up.

I'm not saying those types of decisions are for everyone, just as hiking the AT is not. But we all can learn from their example. They at least have been willing to step into the arena and commit themselves to the fight.

Maybe for you it's committing yourself to your marriage, to remain together for better or worse, and really meaning it; or maybe it's a commitment to graduate from college, or to stop smoking.

Regardless of what it may be, the principle remains the same. You've got to be willing to keep going, no matter how hard you're hit. When things get tough, you must remain committed to your decision. And, like the pig, you must be willing to give it your all. Because if you do, you can't be stopped.

COMMITMENT

*"Until one's committed, there is
hesitancy, the chance to draw
back, always ineffectiveness.
Concerning all acts of initiative
and creation, there is one
elementary truth the ignorance of
which kills countless ideas and
splendid plans: that the moment
one definitely commits oneself,
then providence moves too.*

*All sorts of things occur to help
one that would never otherwise
have occurred. A whole stream of
events issues from the decision,
raising in one's favor all manner
of unforeseen incidents, meetings
and material assistance which no
man could have dreamed would
have come his way. Whatever you
can do or dream you can, begin it.
Boldness has genius, power and
magic in it. Begin it now."*

—JOHANN WOLFGANG VON GOETHE

LESSON FOUR

NEVER QUIT

Hurricane at 5,000 Feet

HURRICANE AT 5,000 FEET

"A 'never quit' attitude is what keeps you going when almost every fiber of your being wants to give up, or when others say 'it' can't be done."

—JAY "PATCH" PLATT

What's one trait that the truly successful share? Although some might argue that it is their background, education, or status, I disagree. Rather, I believe that if you were to study the lives of anyone whose made a mark in this world, you'd find one common denominator that exists—it's their attitude, particularly, their attitude of perseverance.

They quite simply refuse to give up. They are overcomers. They continue when others quit. As a result, they've been able to rise to the top of their respective fields.

Without a doubt, one of the greatest examples of perseverance is none other than Abraham Lincoln. If you want to learn about someone who simply refused to quit, look no further.

Born into poverty, Lincoln was faced with defeat throughout his life. Over the years he lost eight elections, twice failed in business, and suffered a nervous breakdown. Although he could have quit many times, he didn't, and because he didn't, he became one of the greatest presidents in the history of our country.

"Our greatest glory is not in never failing, but in rising up every time we fail."

—RALPH WALDO EMERSON

Or look at Thomas Edison, who invented the incandescent light bulb, but only after over 10,000 unsuccessful attempts. A famous story recounts the time a young reporter asked Edison how it felt to have failed so many times, in his quest to create the light bulb. How was he able to go on? Edison replied, "I haven't failed 10,000 times, I've discovered 10,000 ways that won't work."

Another great example of perseverance is the story of Earl Shaffer who, in 1948, became the first man ever to thru-hike the Appalachian Trail. He did so in spite of the fact that he was told that it was impossible. He chose not to listen to what others said and believed in himself.

At the time of his hike, the trail was a far cry from what it is today. There were places where there was no obvious trail at all, just wilderness, and he had to dead reckon and use a compass to continue. He finished the trail, from Georgia to Maine, in around four months. It was such an unbelievable accomplishment that people didn't even believe he had done it until someone else did the same the following year.

While those are great examples of perseverance, what about you? How's your attitude? Are you one of the ones that get going when the going gets tough or do you instead roll over and give up? Do you have bulldog determination, or is retreat always an option for you?

These are important questions to ask yourself and then answer honestly. I firmly believe that of all the characteristics one needs to be successful in life, a "never quit" attitude is one of the most important. It's what keeps you going when almost every fiber of your being wants to quit, or when others say "it" can't be done.

Unfortunately, far too many people don't possess this of type of attitude. As soon as they get knocked down, they throw in the towel. They never realize their true potential because they quit as soon as things get tough.

My wish is that people would realize that there is light at the end of the tunnel. It doesn't matter how many times you get knocked down as long as you get back up. After each rain storm there's always a rainbow, but to see it, you've got to first go through the storm. The secret is sticking around long enough to see it come to pass.

Although I was already a strong believer in the importance of attitude before my thru-hike, hiking the trail reinforced in me the vital role a proper attitude plays. I never would have made it without it.

The entire trail was difficult at times, but some parts were definitely harder than others. For me, the White Mountains of New Hampshire, and particularly Mt. Madison, tested my attitude to the fullest.

"My sun sets to rise again."

—ROBERT BROWNING

My first taste of the Whites was on a mountain range known as the Wildcats. The Wildcats gave me an indication of just how tough the White Mountains were going to be.

My first day there, while coming down what was basically the face of a cliff, I suddenly had a dizzy spell and slipped and fell sideways. I began to tumble down the mountain until a tree broke my fall. I slammed into a sharp branch that was just a few inches off the ground. My head hit it full force in the area of my left temple, and I blacked out momentarily.

Eventually, I regained my awareness and slowly stood back up. To say it scared me would be the understatement of the century. Shaken at the thought of how close I'd come to a fatal fall, it took several hours from that point for me to make my way down the mountain.

That night was a time of some serious self-reflection. For the first time since I'd begun the hike, I questioned what I was doing and why.

Was I even physically able to accomplish such a feat? Plenty of people were telling me that the answer to that question was no. Maybe they were right. After all, here I was with one eye and a brain tumor, going up and down what at times was downright treacherous terrain.

It was time for a gut check. Was all this attitude stuff that I was always telling others about for real? After thinking awhile, I realized that by completing my hike I had a great opportunity to set an example for others to follow. I realized that by not quitting, even though it was hard, I might one day inspire others to continue during their own tough times. At that point I made the decision that no matter what I wasn't going to quit. I would persevere to the end! I just didn't know how hard it would get.

The next day, although the weather report forecast bad weather and extremely high winds, I climbed Mount Madison with some fellow hikers named Felix, Pokey-Hontas, Soy Boy and Stoat. We all took off together but somehow got separated along the way.

The climb up Madison was tough and steep. It took me several hours of steady climbing to even get near the top. The terrain up there is surreal, like being on another planet or something. It's gravelly surface is packed with huge boulders and remnants of an ancient, volcanic eruption. Also, there are no trees once you get above 4,000 feet or so. And no trees, of course, means that there's nothing to block the wind—which was blowing like crazy!

As I got closer to the summit, I was unsure of the whereabouts of the others. The only other hiker I could see at this point was Felix, stopped about a half of a mile ahead of me.

By the time I was within a quarter of a mile of him, the wind was now easily gusting at 60 to 70 miles per hour. This made it difficult to make much progress.

To move forward, I'd wait for the wind to die down and then would move as quickly as possible. When it began gusting again, I'd get down behind a rock until it had passed. I leapfrogged in this manner until I got to where he was.

Once I reached him, I asked where everyone else was. He said they'd apparently taken the alternate route around the mountain, due to the inclement weather. As a result, he and I were the only ones up there.

After a short break we continued up the mountain. By the time we were within sight of the summit, the temperature had dropped noticeably and the winds were now sustained. They were blowing what must have been at least 90 to 100 mph. It was like being in a hurricane in freezing weather.

To make matters worse there was nowhere to hide from the elements. The only option was to keep moving, but the high winds made it nearly impossible to do so. Finally, at the highest point of the mountain, we found some cover behind a huge boulder. Leaning behind it, I quickly reached into my pack to get some warmer clothes.

As I was putting them on, Felix said that he was going to push on. When I looked back up, he was gone. So there I was, all alone, sitting behind a boulde, on top of a mountain in hurricane force winds.

At this point, all I wanted to do was stay where I was. I was terrified that I'd be blown over the edge if I moved, but I was even more afraid that I'd freeze to death if I didn't. I knew that the winds would remain and the only way to get out of this situation was to take action.

I said a prayer and then left the cover of the rock. I struggled to move an inch at a time. I was blown sideways and fell several times, but kept moving forward.

After what seemed like an eternity, I finally caught a glimpse of a lodge about a half of a mile down. About the same time, the winds let up a bit, and I was able to make it down the mountain.

Though chances are good you'll never personally have to face hurricane force winds on top of a mountain, you will undoubtedly have your own storms in life to face. Your attitude will determine how you come through them.

Resolve now that you'll never give up no matter what may come your way. Just as others have faced tough times and survived them, so can you. It's your decision. As Winston Churchill said, "Never, never, never, never, quit!"

PERSISTENCE

*"Nothing in the world can take
the place of persistence.*

*Talent will not; nothing is more
common than unsuccessful men
with talent.*

*Genius will not; unrewarded it's
almost a proverb*

*Education will not; the world is
filled with educated derelicts.*

*Persistence and determination
alone are omnipotent."*

—CALVIN COOLIDGE

BE FAIR TO ALL

Don't Judge a Book...

DON'T JUDGE A BOOK...

*"...count your blessings, and
while you're at it, treat others like
they're just as special as you..."*

—JAY "PATCH" PLATT

Don't judge a book by its cover. It's an old cliché that most of us have often heard over the years. But how many of us have really taken it to heart? Have you? Or do you allow your perception of others to influence how you treat them? Think about it for a moment. How do you look at the world around you? Do you treat everyone fairly?

When you see a homeless person on the street, what's your first thought? Do you see him or her as a person in need of some help? Do you realize that you too could be in their shoes, if things went wrong in your life? Or, do you just look at them with disgust in your eyes? Are they just lazy bums? Do you wonder why they don't just get a job? Things to think about, huh?

What about someone who's overweight? They couldn't have any pride in themselves, right? I mean, why don't they just exercise and diet? They probably don't have the discipline you have, do they? Or what about the...?

I could go on and on, but I think you get the picture.

The reality is, the majority of us don't treat others as fairly as we should. Particularly when they're not like us. Most of us, it seems, are prejudiced in one way or another, whether we admit it out loud or not.

We tend to believe that we're somehow better than those who are less fortunate than us, or different from us. This type of thinking is universal too. All races, genders, religions, etc., can be subject to a certain amount of prejudice, according to where you are in the world.

One important point to remember about prejudice, however, is that it's a behavior—and like all behaviors, it's something that we're taught.

If you look at young children, you'll notice that they accept everyone. It's not until they are influenced by others that they begin to hate those around them.

The positive side of this is that just as we can be taught negative behavior, we can also be taught positive ways to act.

Looking back on my own life, I must confess that I can rarely recall a time when I felt like I was being looked down upon by others.

Sure, growing up, I was teased at times, as I'm sure everyone is. But I can never recall a time when I felt like I was being looked down on by others, because of who or what they perceived me to be.

Why is that? Well, to be quite honest, in this country, I've had it made. Being a white male in America, I've been privileged to acceptance by most of society. I'm not saying that's right, it's just the way it is. When you look like the majority, and act like the majority, then you're usually accepted by the majority. And that's where I stood, until the AT.

As a thru-hiker, for the first time in my life, I experienced discrimination, and, I must admit, I didn't like it! This discrimination didn't come from my fellow hikers but from others in society.

It seems that I no longer fit into the mold of how you're supposed to act, look, smell, etc. I guess my scraggly beard, dirty clothing and the black patch I wore over my left eye weren't exactly people magnets.

While my appearance was perfectly acceptable on the trail with other hikers, it was far from it around non-hikers. More often than not, when I was in a town, at a restaurant, in a store, or even on the street, I'd get the distinct feeling that I wasn't welcome.

One of the first instances of this occurred in New Hampshire. I'd just arrived in the first major town I'd visited in over a month of being on the trail. I couldn't wait to get there. I was so hungry for something other than trail food and was really looking forward to a hot shower.

Shortly after arriving in town, my buddy Felix and I came across a Dunkin Donuts. Dunkin Donuts! Wow! I couldn't wait to get my hands on some freshly made donuts. I could just see myself easily eating a dozen, all by my lonesome.

Then it happened. As I was getting ready to place my order, the cashier asked me a question that caught me by surprise. She said, "It's a little early for Halloween, isn't it?"

Now in all honesty, I'll admit that comment didn't really hurt my feelings that badly. I learned a long time ago that what others think about you is really irrelevant. The only thing that really matters is what you think of yourself. But her flippant remark was insensitive to say the least, so I decided to make her "pay" for her comment.

I acted like I'd been devastated by her remark. I told her it had taken me over a year to build up the courage to leave my house after the loss of my eye. I explained how worried I'd been about what others would think about my appearance. I continued by telling her that only after finally being convinced by my family that the patch really wasn't that noticeable had I decided to face the public again.

"Judge not, that you not be judged. For with what judgment you judge, you will be judged; and with the measure you use it will be measured back to you."

—MATTHEW 7: 1-3

By now, I could tell that I'd made her feel pretty low. But I went on and told her that I felt that she'd discriminated against me.

About this time, Felix caught on to what I was doing and began trying to "console" me. At this point, the lady began apologizing like crazy. She even offered to give us our donuts for free— and we took her up on her offer.

I was harassed in a similar fashion a couple other times while on the trail. Once, while in a restaurant, a man asked me if I was supposed to be Captain Hook or something. Another time, a man pointed at me and said to his son, "Look son, it's a woods pirate."

Now, I'll be the first to admit that on the surface these comments seem harmless enough. But on the other hand, I believe they are reflective of a growing trend in our society of not caring about the feelings of others.

I couldn't help but think of how someone must feel when they're made fun of because they talk, walk, or look differently.

Other sorts of subtle discrimination occurred any time I would go into a restaurant. I'd have to wait forever to be seated and then only in a corner away from everyone else. Getting decent service was nearly impossible, and many times the service was downright rude. All of these examples are minor, though, compared to what happened to me in Pennsylvania.

I'd hiked for fifteen miles one day and decided to camp beside a road for the night. The night went by without incident. But the next morning I woke up with blurred vision in my right eye that was steadily getting worse. This wasn't a good situation to be in, period, but especially as a one-eyed man.

I was immediately concerned because I went blind in my left eye under similar circumstances. I was worried that the disease might have now moved into my right eye. I gathered up my gear and staggered across the road to a parking lot. Because it was Sunday, I figured there would be people coming by to hike in the area for the day.

Sure enough, not long after, an elderly couple pulled up. By this time, my right eye was in a lot of pain. I cupped my hand over it to block out the sunlight and staggered over to their car. I waved hello and motioned them to roll down the window. The lady cracked her window just an inch.

I explained to them that I was a hiker and had hurt my eye and needed some help. Their response? They told me to leave them alone and sped off.

I couldn't believe it. But after thinking about it, I decided that I probably looked pretty scary to them. They probably just didn't understand what I wanted. The next time I'd try to be a little more calm and articulate what I needed.

About thirty minutes later, a man and his son pulled up in a pick-up truck. They got out and walked my way. When they got beside me I said, "Excuse me sir. I know I look a mess, but I'm not a bum. I'm a thru-hiker and I need your help. You see, I've got this form of cancer that caused me to go blind in my left eye, and I'm afraid it's now moved into my right eye. I can barely see anything out of it. I really don't know what else to do. Could you please help me?"

After explaining like that, I thought surely he'd help me. But he didn't. He just told me that he wasn't going my way and to leave them alone. I couldn't believe it. I was outraged! More than that, though, I was saddened by the example that he was setting for his son, who was watching every move his father made.

Now, I was seriously getting worried. What if no one would help me? I realized that there wasn't anything else I could do about the situation, so I then put it in someone's hands that could. I said a prayer and asked God to please send someone my way who would be willing to help me. Within five minutes, a Jeep Cherokee pulled up. Out came a couple, who were about to do a day-hike in the area.

As they approached, I asked if one of them could look at my right eye for me. She, (her name was Susan) looked at it and said she didn't see anything stuck in it. They then asked me if I needed a lift somewhere. Another prayer answered! They drove me about fifteen miles, and dropped me off at a hotel, near an interstate.

As soon as I got in my room, I lay down and slept for several hours. When I woke up, my eye was fine, though bloodshot red. Apparently, whatever was in it had worked its way out while I slept.

The next day, I was faced with the dilemma of determining where I was, and how to get back to the trail. Across the road from the hotel was a convenience store. Figuring they'd have a map of the area, I went in to take a look.

Just as I'd guessed, over in one corner of the store were dozens of maps. As I was browsing through one of them, the clerk asked me what I was doing. I explained that I was just browsing. She then said that if I wasn't going to buy anything, I'd have to leave the store. She didn't stop there, though. She went on to say that if I didn't leave, she was going to call the police. I couldn't believe this was happening.

She didn't know me or anything about me. She just assumed things about me, because of my appearance. I was so furious that I told her to do what she had to do because I wasn't leaving until I was good and ready.

All of these incidents taught me great deal about human behavior. I was able to get a glimpse of what it must feel like to be a member of an unaccepted minority.

In all fairness I must admit that there were also many, many good people that I met on the trail—people who picked me up in the rain, people who opened their homes up to me, etc. To them, I'm forever indebted.

But I think I learned the most from the bad examples I saw because they reminded me of something that we all should keep in mind—that none of us, not one, is more special than the other. Sadly, many people forget that fact. They don't seem to realize that it was only by a blessing that they've arrived where they are today.

Think about it. What makes you more special than a child in India or Somalia that is starving? What did you do to deserve to not have muscular dystrophy? Why weren't you born mentally retarded?

My point is this: You had no control over those things—and neither did they. You were just blessed. The best thing you can do is count your blessings, and while you're at it, treat others like they're just as special as you, because I'll tell you a secret—they are.

WHO COUNTS?

"It is not the critic who counts, nor the man who points out how the strong man stumbles, or where the doer of deeds could have done better. The credit belongs to the man who is actually in the arena; whose face is marred by dust and sweat; who strives valiantly; who errs and may fail again, because there is no effort without error or shortcoming, but who does actually strive to do the deeds; who does know the great enthusiasm, the great devotion; who spends himself in a worthy cause; who at best, knows in the end the triumph of high achievement, and who at worst, if he fails, at least fails while daring greatly, so that his place shall never be with those cold and timid souls who know neither victory nor defeat."

—THEODORE ROOSEVELT

LESSON SIX

LISTEN TO OTHERS

Five Minutes

FIVE MINUTES

*"In the wake of all the shootings,
suicides, and drug abuse that
we're now experiencing in this
country, how many people just
need someone to listen? Maybe,
all they need is five minutes."*

—JAY "PATCH" PLATT

F ive minutes. Not a lot of time it
seems. But as I was to learn on the
trail, five minutes can mean a lot.

A Marine buddy of mine, named
Ron, joined me in Pennsylvania to hike with me
for a week or so. The plan was for us to hike to
Maryland and then have my wife, Paz, meet us
there and give Ron a ride back home.

Our hike went well. It was great having some company for a week, and Ron and I were able to talk about old times. At the end of the week, we did a sixteen miler, and came to an intersection of the trail and a road that led into the town where we were meeting Paz at the following day.

Tired, dirty and hungry, we intended to get into town as quickly as possible, clean up, and then go get some chow. Unfortunately, the town was three miles away. If we walked it, we were looking at it taking at least an hour. Neither of us looked forward to the proposition of walking three more miles that day. Our hope was that maybe someone would stop and give us a ride.

As poor luck would have it, while we were standing there a cold, drizzling rain began to fall. With the rain and all, we figured there was no way someone would stop for us, so we began walking towards town. We hadn't been walking long when, unexpectedly, a big four-wheeler pulled up beside us.

The driver rolled down the window nearest me and introduced himself as C.J. Peering into the vehicle, I immediately took note of a 30-caliber rifle sitting in its gun rack and a big black dog riding shotgun.

C.J. was dressed in hunting clothes and had about a week's worth of growth on his face. The smell of a combination of whiskey, cigarettes, and coffee was evident from where we stood.

Ron and I introduced ourselves and explained to him that we were hikers and needed a ride into town. After looking us over for a moment, he said, "Okay sure, no problem," and told us to throw our gear into the back of the pickup. He asked where we wanted to go exactly and I told him the nearest motel would be fine.

As we were getting into the back of the truck, Ron yelled, "OohRah!" Upon hearing that, C.J. asked, "What did you just say?" Ron replied, "Oh it's nothing; just Marine talk I guess. It's just something we Marines say when we're motivated." C.J. began to nod his head in the affirmative, and his eyes lit up, as he too said, "OohRah!"

You could hear the excitement in his voice as he leapt out of the truck and came over to where we were with his right hand extended. As he shook both of our hands, he explained that he too had been a Marine. He'd been out of the Corps for over thirteen years and hadn't heard someone say "Oohrah" since. Ron let him know that he was an active duty Gunnery Sergeant, and I piped in that I, too, was a Marine, recently retired.

Now that he knew we were Marines, he insisted that we go get some beer and take it to his house. Then we could talk about the good old days.

Initially, I declined. The last thing I wanted to do was to go over to some guy's house and party all night. I was tired and dirty. All I wanted to do was get myself a room with a tub and plenty of hot water, a bed, and maybe a television set. But C.J. was adamant. He went on and on about how much more room there was, and how much more comfortable we'd be at his house than in any motel.

Reluctantly, I gave in after his mention of his wife and two kids. I figured that with his family there, things wouldn't get out of hand, and maybe we'd even get a home-cooked meal. Little did I know how wrong I was!

It didn't take long after arriving at his house, to realize that "We weren't in Kansas anymore."

He led us into the house through the garage and immediately took us into the basement. He told us to remain there while he went to "check things out," which struck me as peculiar. He returned a few minutes later and informed us that all was clear. I asked where his wife and kids were.

"The old lady's working and won't be home until ten o'clock or so, and the kids are with their grandparents for the night," he explained.

He went on, "We've got the house to ourselves, but you've got to hide downstairs when my wife gets home. Keep the lights out and make sure you don't make a sound."

Now, I thought, this was getting downright weird, as the theme from *The Twilight Zone* began playing in my head. I started to ask him about all the secrecy, but decided to just let it go, although I was rapidly beginning to regret my decision of coming there. As strange as all of this was, it would get a lot stranger before this night was done.

After stowing our gear downstairs, we met C.J. in the kitchen. I used the phone to call my wife. We talked for a few minutes, made plans to meet the next day, then said goodbye. Shortly after I hung up, the phone rang. It was C.J.'s wife. She wanted to know why the phone had been busy. He explained to her that he'd met a couple of fellow Marines who were hiking the AT and had invited them over. But she didn't want to listen.

She was obviously upset with the whole situation, and an argument ensued. Back and forth they went. After about five minutes of this, he handed the phone to Ron and said, "She wants to talk to you, and it don't sound good." With a surprised look on his face, Ron took the phone and said, "Hello?" This was followed by a minute or so of him saying, "Yes ma'am, Yes ma'am, Yes ma'am."

After Ron hung up the phone, I asked him what was said. He replied, "She said that we have five minutes to be out of her house before she calls the law."

I told Ron I thought our leaving was probably for the best. When C.J. heard this, he became irate. He said there was no way we were leaving. We weren't going anywhere until he had a chance to talk to us.

"Look," I said, "we don't want to get you in any trouble with your wife and we definitely don't want any trouble with the police."

Ignoring my comment, he sat down, popped open a beer and began to tell of his days in the Marine Corps. He'd been drinking pretty heavily by this time, so the stories flowed out easily.

After listening awhile, it became obvious to Ron and me that, as a Marine, he'd been less than a stellar performer. He'd been in and out of trouble while in the Corps, and had received a bad conduct discharge as a result. His luck as a civilian hadn't been much better, as he'd been unable to hold down a job.

He went on to say that he'd served as a scout-sniper in Panama and had five confirmed kills there. Now, whether that story was true or not I don't know, but to him it was very real. As he spoke about it, his eyes glazed over and he began to stare blankly into space.

Suddenly, he got up and went into the other room. He returned carrying a framed article from the local newspaper. It was about a break-in which had occurred in the area the year before. The homeowner had defended his residence by shooting the burglar in the chest with a .357 magnum pistol. The wounded man had died as a result of the gunshot wounds en route to the hospital. The shooter had been C.J.

He described how he'd shot the guy several times in the chest. He then admitted that he had been unable to get it out of his mind ever since. Then, in an instant, from under his shirt, he pulled out a handgun and laid it on the table in front of him! I could tell that it was a semi-automatic pistol with the magazine inserted. He began pushing its nose, causing it to spin on the

table. He said he sometimes felt like just ending
it all. He didn't know where to turn. If only
someone would listen to him. "No one ever lis-
tens to me!" he screamed. "All I want is five
minutes."

I've got to admit, I was about as scared at
that moment as I'd ever been. In an instant, my
life flashed before me. I thought about all that
I'd been through over the years.

I couldn't believe what was now happening.
I'd spent over fourteen years in the Marine
Corps, had fought a chronic disease for years,
and had faced plenty of challenges on the AT
over the last few months. Could it be possible
that I was now about to face some lunatic with a
loaded gun?

As I pondered what to do next, just as
quickly as he'd removed it, he placed the gun
back under his shirt and calmly asked if we were
hungry. Neither Ron nor I wanted to freak this
guy out, so as strange as it sounds, we acted as if
nothing had happened and went ahead and ate
some dinner—bear meat and potatoes, of all
things!

During dinner, we were able to talk more.
Actually, we mostly just let him talk, while we
listened. He obviously just needed to get some
things off his chest. As he did, his whole

demeanor changed, and he became much calmer.

After we'd finished eating, the phone rang. It was his wife. She wanted to know if we'd left yet as she'd instructed. C.J. was now much more relaxed as he spoke to her. He promised her that he'd take us into town right away. He then gave us a ride to the nearest motel.

As we were saying our good-byes, C.J. said he wanted to thank us for everything. He went on to tell us that, although we didn't know it, we'd probably saved his life that night. Five minutes before he ran into us, he'd given up on his life. All he was thinking about was how he couldn't go on anymore. But, after spending five minutes with us, he knew that he could.

He then got right in my face. Eye to eye, nose to nose. I wasn't sure what to think. Then, with tears in his eyes, he wrapped his arms around me, and hugged me tightly.

I, like your typical man, just stood there with my arms straight down by my sides. And then he said, "I love you, man." He went on, "This is the best night I've had since leaving the Corps. You're the first Marines I've been with in all that time. Thanks for listening."

As I hugged him back like I would my brother, I said, "I love you, too, man. Semper Fidelis."

That night taught me a valuable lesson on the importance of listening. I'm not so naïve as to believe that all C.J. needed to fix his ills was the time he spent with us. Undoubtedly, he needs some professional help.

I do believe, however, that we were able to divert what could have been a tragedy that night simply by listening to him. And that makes me wonder.

In the wake of all the shootings, suicides, and drug abuse that we're now experiencing in this country, how many people just need someone to listen to them? Maybe all they need is five minutes.

DON'T QUIT

When things go wrong as they sometimes will, and the road you're trudging seems all up hill. When the funds are low and the debts are high, and you want to smile, but you have to sigh. When care is pressing you down a bit, rest if you must, but don't you quit.

Life is queer with its twists and turns, as every one of us sometimes learns. And many a failure turns about, when he might have won, had he stuck it out. Don't give up, though the pace seems slow, you may succeed with another blow.

Success is failure turned inside out, the silver tint of the clouds of doubt. And you never can tell how close you are, it may be near, when it seems so far. So stick to the fight, when you're hardest hit. It's when things seem worst, that you must not quit.

—UNKNOWN

LESSON SEVEN

FACE YOUR FEARS

Rat Attack

RAT ATTACK

"So commit now, that the next time you're faced with a fear, you'll stand up to it. It's the surest way to guarantee its death."

—JAY "PATCH" PLATT

The week before I left for Maine to begin my thru-hike, I watched the movie, "The Edge." In case you haven't seen it, it's about some guys whose plane crashes in a remote area of Alaska. They then have to survive and find a way out. In the process, they end up being stalked by a ferocious grizzly bear.

It's a great movie, but probably not a good one to see just before leaving for a six-month stint in the wilderness.

Around the same time, I read an article in *Back Packer* magazine about black bears. The article said that black bears, although smaller, can be even more dangerous than grizzlies.

These two events sparked a growing fear in me of the proposition of my meeting a hungry bear late one night. Knowing I'd be alone and without any sort of weapon didn't reassure me any.

As it turned out, I never actually saw a bear during my entire hike (although I did see many signs of their presence). That doesn't mean I didn't have to deal with my share of fear while out there.

I had many run-ins with all sorts of wild animals—moose, deer, coyote, and snakes. But of all the encounters I had, one night sticks out more than all the rest. It's a night I won't soon forget.

That day began like any other. I'd stayed in the small town of Troutville, Virginia, the night before. Typical of most of my town visits, it was after noon before I finally tore myself away and forced myself to begin hiking. The hiking seemed harder than usual that day, but most of that was probably due to the full belly I left with.

After several hours of hiking, I came upon Lambert's Meadow Shelter, just before sundown. *The Thru-Hikers' Handbook* gave a warning to be careful at this shelter for copperhead snakes. There'd been numerous sightings of them in the rocks around the firepit, and in the crevices of the stone building.

By the time I set my gear up for the night, got my water and cooked dinner it was almost completely dark. After dinner, I continued reading a book I'd begun a week before entitled, *The Power of Positive Living* by Dr. Vincent Normal Peale. It's a really powerful book.

I was at a point in the book where Dr. Peale discusses fear and ways to overcome it. He details the many ways in which fear holds us back from being all that we can be in our lives.

The book conveys the vital importance of conquering fear and then gives some excellent advice on how to do so.

One point which really stood out for me, was when he said that the surest way to ensure the death of fear is to face up to it.

I remember thinking about how much sense that made. I promised myself that the next fearful situation I came upon, I'd simply face it and see if it went away. I didn't realize how quickly I'd have the opportunity.

"Fear defeats more people than any other one thing in the world."

—RALPH WALDO EMERSON

I'd just set the book down and was getting ready for bed, when I heard something crashing through the woods. Whatever it was, was big, and it wasn't alone. It sounded like three or four of them were coming my way. My immediate thought was, "Oh no, that must be a group of bears!" Then, I remembered my promise.

Although it took me several minutes to do so, I finally gathered up my courage. With a flashlight in one hand, and a stick in the other, I stepped out of the shelter. Slowly, ever so slowly, I crept into the pitch black darkness, toward the sound of the footsteps.

As I got closer to the noise, my heart was beating so fast that I thought it was going to explode from my chest. Then a funny thing happened.

The animals must have sensed my presence and took off running in the opposite direction, away from the shelter. As soon as I heard them running away, I let out a war cry and yelled, "And stay away!"

Man, was I ever proud. I'd faced up to my fear and won. I strutted back to the shelter, patting myself on the back for being so brave. But my challenge wasn't over yet.

Just as I was about to step into the shelter, I heard a sound that made my heart stand still momentarily. The best way I can describe it, is to compare it to a witch's laugh—like the wicked witch in "The Wizard of Oz."

As I turned toward the sound, I fully expected to find some hideously warted, green faced sorceress, wearing a pointy hat and shoes, intent on casting a spell on me.

Instead, I found two green eyes, about one and a half feet off the ground, staring at me, as they approached my position. Without hesitation, I lunged toward the creature, yelling at the top of my lungs. This startled it, and it took off running into the woods, from whence it came.

Now, my head was really swelled with bravado. I'd faced up to two fears that night, and was victorious in both.

After sufficiently bragging a bit to myself about how truly brave I'd been, I decided it was time to turn in for the evening.

The truth of the matter is, I prayed that these two events would be the extent of my "tests" for the night. But that wasn't to be the case.

As I was getting situated inside my sleeping bag, I heard something, making a commotion up in the rafters of the shelter. I tried to ignore it, but my curiosity finally got the best of me.

I got out of my bag, turned on my flashlight, and walked over to the area that I'd heard the noise.

I still, to this day, can't believe what I saw. Although I'm convinced that I'll never be able to fully and accurately describe the sight, I'll still give it my best shot here.

Let me preface this description, by saying that, having grown up in rural South Georgia, I very well know what both an opossum and a raccoon looks like. This thing was neither.

What I saw that night, was unbelievable. I'm not sure how big an average rat gets, but this thing was beyond huge! It must have been, at least, a foot and a half long, and weighed over twenty-five pounds. To make matters worse, it was actually snarling at me (something I didn't know rats did).

To say the least, I was unhappy with seeing this rat, especially after some of the stories I'd heard about hikers encountering them.

One guy had told me a story about something that happened to him in the Smoky Mountains. He was awakened one night by something pulling on his hair. When he looked to see what it was, he discovered several rats surrounding him. One of them had pieces of his hair in its mouth. (Apparently, they use the hair to make their nest.) He had to fight them off all night long.

Someone else had told me that rats will try to get into your sleeping bag with you for warmth. Trust me, I definitely didn't want any company in my sleeping bag that night!

As I moved closer, the rat backed down, but I had an eerie feeling that this was going to be an all night battle.

After not hearing any sign of it for about fifteen minutes, I lay back down. Then, shortly after I dozed off, it made it' move again.

This time I got up and tried to hit it with one of my hiking sticks. I swung, and it ducked. "This is war!" I declared.

Then, in an instant, the odds turned toward the rat's favor—the bulb in my flashlight blew!

I stood there in complete darkness. There was no moon that night, and my eye was victim to sudden night blindness. I knew from experience that it would take at least thirty minutes to regain some sense of night vision.

Now, I don't know if you'd call this luck, or fate, or just great intuition, but I'd recently began carrying a candle and lighter in my coat pocket. As I had no other flashlight bulbs with me, the candle would have to serve me until morning.

I made use of that candle many, many times that night. Repeatedly, throughout the night, the rat tried to get to me and my bag.

Every time it would get near me, I'd light the candle and then swing like crazy, in the rat's direction, with my hiking stick. Although I connected a couple of times, the rat kept coming. This went on until daybreak. As you can imagine, it was a very long night.

"The only thing we have to fear is fear itself."

—FRANKLIN DELANO ROOSEVELT

Though chances are good that you'll never have to face a giant rat like I did that night; you will undoubtedly, at some point, have to face fear in your life. The fact is, everyone fears something. Some people are just too afraid to admit it.

Is all fear bad? Of course not. Sometimes it's wise to listen to your "gut" feeling about something. This type of fear just might save your life.

For instance, if you have a fear of jumping into a fire, it's probably smart to listen to it. It's totally rational. If you didn't have such a fear and jumped into the fire, chances are you'd be badly burned.

Therefore, this type of rational fear makes perfect sense. It's been programmed into us to keep us safe. There are many other examples of rational fear, but I won't belabor the point because I'm sure you get the idea. Instead, I want to concentrate on those fears that have no rational basis.

These irrational fears are the ones that remain unseen to others, but that you know you have. They can be dangerous, if not stood up to. They have the ability to ruin one's life, or, at a minimum, to keep one from living life to the fullest.

A common example of this type of fear is the feeling of utter and complete terror that grips many people when they have to speak in front of a group.

While such a fear isn't rational—after all nothing bad is going to happen to you just because you speak in front of a group—it is still as paralyzing, for many, as the fear of jumping in a fire is. Why would someone feel this way?

Such an irrational fear is actually rooted in something much deeper than may appear on the surface. I believe it's part of a bigger fear, one that is more detrimental than all the others combined.

This fear is so prevalent that it's evident in almost epidemic proportions throughout our society. It's the root cause from which many other fears spring.

Actually, this fear is the driving force in many peoples' lives. It has the ability to prevent you from ever truly reaching your potential. Because of it, hopes and dreams are never acted upon, and it often causes good people to do bad things in their lives.

So what fear do I speak of? THE FEAR OF WHAT OTHERS THINK. Think about it. Why do you think young people try drugs? With all of the education, it's certainly not because they don't know they're bad for them. It's not because they haven't been told to just say NO! The reason is, they're more concerned with what their peers think of the, than anything else. It's the same thing with premarital sex and virtually any other problem teens face.

Unfortunately, adults aren't much better. Most still allow the fear of what others think to rule their lives. They don't dare do something which would make them stand out from the norm. They refuse to do anything which might embarrass them, so they usually do nothing at all.

This is why so many people don't extend themselves in social situations, are terrified at the thought of meeting someone new or having to speak in front of a group.

The ironic thing about this fear is that while we're worrying what others are thinking about us, chances are they're doing the same.

I truly believe that if a person could just get over this one fear, they could do virtually anything. They'd be unstoppable! It just takes the decision to do so and then the courage to follow through on that decision.

Will it be easy? Probably not. But each time you don't cower to what you're afraid of, you become more powerful to fight it the next time—until you finally defeat it.

So commit now that the next time you're faced with such a fear, you'll stand up to it. It's the surest way to guarantee its death. Now get up, and go face your rat!

It's The Man Who Thinks He Can

If you think you are beaten, you are,
If you think you dare not, you don't.
If you like to win, but you think you can't,
It is almost certain you won't.

If you think you'll lose, you're lost,
For out in the world we find,
Success begins with a fellow's will.
It's all in the state of mind.

If you think you are outclassed, you are,
You've got to think high to rise,
You've got to be sure of yourself before

You can ever win a prize.

Life's battles don't always go
to the stronger or faster man.
But soon or late the man who wins,
Is the man who thinks he can.

—Unknown

LESSON EIGHT

SET GOALS

One Day, I'll...

ONE DAY, I'LL...

> *"With very few exceptions, nothing's ever going to be totally perfect. If you're waiting for everything to be just right before you set out on a goal, you may be waiting a long time."*
>
> —JAY "PATCH" PLATT

One day, I'll..." How many of us have spoken those words only to have them never come true? "I'll do it when I graduate from school," or "I'll do it when I pay off the bills," or "I'll do it when the kids are grown," or "I'll do it when..." Basically, what we're saying is that we'll do "it" when everything is just right. The truth is that day usually never comes. It's not that we don't intend to follow through. We just allow life to get in the way.

A perfect example of this is the story of an eighty-five year old couple who had been engaged since age twenty. They'd come to a young preacher and asked him to marry them. He replied that he'd be glad to, but just had to know one thing: "Why did you wait so long before you decided to tie the knot?"

"Well," they replied, "We were waiting for everything to be just right before the wedding, but after sixty-five years, we've come to the conclusion that that day will never come."

As funny as that story is, it's how many people actually live their lives. The reality is, with very few exceptions, nothing is ever going to be totally perfect. If you are waiting for everything to be just right before you set out on a goal, you may be waiting a long time. Usually, it's best to follow the advice of the Nike company and "Just do it."

If I had waited for the perfect time to thru-hike the Appalachian Trail, I would probably still be waiting. I didn't have the proper gear, I wasn't in hiking shape, I'd never even visited the trail, and it would be August before I could begin, which meant winter hiking.

The odds certainly weren't in my favor, but I kept remembering a quote by Goethe who said, "Whatever you can do or dream you can, begin it. Boldness has genius, magic, and power in it. Begin it now." With that in mind, I just did it.

"Twenty years from now, you will be more disappointed by the things you didn't do than by the ones you did. So, throw off the bowlines. Sail away from the safe harbor. Catch the trade winds in your sails. Explore. Dream."

—MARK TWAIN

I made my decision to hike in July and was on the trail by August. I didn't overanalyze the process. If I had, I would probably still be getting ready to get ready.

So how do you go about, "just doing it"? By following the process of setting and achieving goals. Let's take a closer look.

The first thing you must do is determine exactly what it is that you'd like to be, do, or have. What are your dreams and desires? No one can answer these questions but you, because each of us is unique.

As you're thinking about these questions, take a notepad and jot down whatever comes to mind. Don't censor your thoughts because they seem too outrageous.

For now, you're simply creating a wish list. Later, we'll discuss how to convert your wishes into doable goals. Remember, with very few exceptions, if you can dream it, you can do it.

Don't fall into the trap of believing that you'll remember or act on your goals without writing them down. The act of putting your thoughts on paper has power in it. The importance of this can't be stressed enough. If you don't write them down, your chance of attaining your goals is diminished greatly.

It's been said that a goal is just a dream with a deadline. The big question then, is how do you go about turning a dream into an achievable goal? There's a really great acronym someone developed, which teaches you to do just that. By following this acronym, all of your goals will be **SMART**.

S Goals must be **specific**. Don't generalize. It's important to say exactly what you want.

For instance, it's not good enough to just say that you want to be a better salesperson. What does that mean exactly? Better than who or what? How will you know when you're better?

Maybe it means that you will increase your take home pay by twenty-five percent or that you will get a promotion. The key thing is to be specific. The more specific you are, the better your chance of accomplishing your goal.

M Goals must be **measurable**. As much as possible, you want to use a yardstick to determine the progress on your goal. Placing a measure on a goal helps you to realize, at any given moment, where you are in that goal's pursuit.

If you're striving to become the salesperson of the year, set up a method of determining your progress. Determine how many sales you need to be making per week, telephone calls per day, etc. This way you're able to track your progress along the way.

A Goals must be **attainable**. Don't set your goals so high that they are unattainable.

For example, say you're a thirty-five-year-old man without a college education. Your chance of becoming an astronaut for NASA, is probably next to none. To set that as a goal is only setting yourself up for failure.

However, you could earn a degree in rocket science and then get a career at NASA as a scientist.

Don't get me wrong. I'm not saying that you shouldn't set your goals high, only that you should set them in such a way that you can attain them.

R Goals must be **realistic**. This step goes hand in hand with step three. If you're unrealistic in setting your goals, you are once again, just setting yourself up for failure.

This is what many people do when wanting to lose weight and the diet industry thrives on it. Even though it took them twenty-one years to gain an extra twenty-one pounds, they believe they can lose it all in twenty-one days. That's just not realistic.

At the end of the three weeks, they see that they haven't reached their goal, so they give up in disgust. If only they had, instead, set a realistic goal of say losing two pounds a month, they would see progress, wouldn't quit, and would eventually reach their goal.

T Goals must be **timely**. You've got to have a deadline. It's not good enough to just say, "One day I'll…"

By having a definite timeline, you're able to keep on track and stay focused. Although it's essential to have a completion date set, it's also important to be flexible and not get too upset if you miss the deadline. Work as hard as you can to make it, but if you miss it, simply set another date and then work toward it.

On my hike, I had to readjust my finish date several times. I'd originally planned to finish by the first of December. But, as I realized that wasn't attainable for me, I reset it for mid December, then again for late January. Even though I didn't make my original date, I did accomplish much more than I ever would have, if I'd just said, "One day I'll..."

Once you've developed your **SMART** goals, the next step is to divide them into short, mid and long-term categories. Generally speaking:

Short-term goals are those that you'd like to accomplish within the next year or so;

Mid-term goals are the ones that you'd like to achieve within the next five to ten years;

Long-term goals are those that you'd like to accomplish which take more than ten years, and could take a lifetime.

Often times, these different categories build upon each other. To get to your long-term goal requires that you, first take certain steps in the short and mid-term.

For instance, let's say your long-term goal is to have a net worth of ten million dollars by age sixty-five. Obviously, you're not going to just wake up one day and have ten million dollars in your account. A goal that large requires you to break it up into smaller chunks.

Some short-term goals here might include beginning an investment program, or if necessary, getting into a line of work or business which will allow you to attain a net worth of that size. These goals in themselves might require you to take additional steps, but I think you get the idea.

Next, using the same example as above, you might have a mid-term goal of having a net worth of five million dollars by age forty-five. This would give you a tangible way of knowing if you're on track to accomplish your long-term goal.

Once you've divided your goals into one of the three categories, prioritize them into no more than the top three that you're willing to commit to.

You'll be much more effective by maintaining your focus this way than you'd ever be by jumping around, dabbling in this and that.

Remember, no matter what your ultimate goal may be, break it down into bite size chunks. As the Chinese philosophy says: "The journey of 1,000 miles begins with a single step."

Once you have determined what goal you're shooting for, visualize yourself achieving it at least three times a day. This will keep it in the forefront of your mind.

However, all the visualization in the world won't help you accomplish your goal if you don't take the most important step, which is working diligently on it each and every day.

Finally, once you've reached the goal you're working on, don't kick back and rest on your laurels. Immediately set out and begin work on another. This is what keeps life interesting. Once you stop trying to get more out of your life, you stop growing. And once you stop growing, you start dying.

I learned a great deal on the subject of setting and achieving goals during my thru-hiking experience. Along the way, I followed some rules that helped me a lot, which you might find helpful in your own pursuits.

Review your goals. Each day I'd review my goals, always keeping in mind what it was I was striving to accomplish.

I'd do so in the morning before I began hiking, again anytime I took a break, and finally, again that evening just before going to sleep. This kept me focused on what I was doing, and thinking about the goal helped tremendously.

In addition to thinking about what I needed to do that day and week to achieve my mileage goal (my short and mid-term goals), I'd also think about how great it was going to be to get to Georgia (my long-term goal).

Visualize success. I always kept a clear picture of what I wanted to accomplish each step along the way, through visualization.

I never allowed myself to think of the possibility of not accomplishing my goal. I only visualized success. No matter how tired, lonesome, or hungry I was, I always pictured myself succeeding. Therefore, I performed as if I could do nothing but succeed.

Focus. Another thing I found to be extremely important, was focusing on each and every step and concentrating most of my energy on where I was at the time.

While it's okay to think about your mid and long-term goals, your main focus still needs to be on the immediate task at hand.

You can't just daydream about how great it's going to be when you finally accomplish your end goal, and expect to attain it. In order to get there, you've got to take the necessary day in and day out steps. That's the only way to accomplish what you've set out to do.

Many people want to skip steps, but it doesn't work like that. I learned that the hard way. There were times during my hike (particularly when I first began) that I literally had to focus on each and every step. That's how small I had to break down my goals. If I didn't, I never would have made it to the end of the day.

It was wet and slippery, and I was falling several times a day. Inevitably, as soon as I'd start daydreaming about finishing the hike, or even finishing for the day, I'd slip and wind up on my back. It didn't take much of this for me to learn to focus on the task at hand!

I'll end this chapter with an exercise. Take the next few minutes and on a blank sheet of paper, write out a wish list of all your hopes, dreams, and desires. Write down everything you'd like to do, be, or have.

Remember, it's imperative that you write down everything that comes to your mind. Don't think about why it can't be done. Just write it down!

Once you have your list together, using the acronym **SMART**, convert your wishes into goals, then go out and begin achieving them!

To get you started, I've given you some suggestions from my own wish list—an ongoing list of things that I'm working on, or intend to work on, that are important to me.

However, keep in mind that, ultimately, you've got to come up with your own list.

Because, chances are, what you and I want out of life are completely different. No one knows what you want out of life but you. It's up to you to get it.

One day I'll...

- ❐ Sightsee in Paris
- ❐ Whale watch in Hawaii
- ❐ Body Surf in Australia
- ❐ Visit the Great Wall of China
- ❐ Learn to ice skate
- ❐ Write a book*
- ❐ Learn to snow ski*
- ❐ Learn to speak Spanish
- ❐ Write a letter to a friend each week
- ❐ Visit the Vatican
- ❐ Canoe down the Amazon
- ❐ Travel to the Holy Land
- ❐ Bench press twice my body weight
- ❐ Meet Les Brown
- ❐ Scuba dive in the Bahamas
- ❐ Run and complete a Marathon

- ❐ Give a food basket to a needy family each Thanksgiving
- ❐ Kayak in Alaska
- ❐ Be a positive role model for others to follow
- ❐ Volunteer at a soup kitchen weekly
- ❐ Learn sign language
- ❐ Learn to fly fish
- ❐ Sponsor a needy child
- ❐ Become a Competent Toastmaster*
- ❐ Give $1,000,000 to charity yearly
- ❐ Thru-hike the AT*
- ❐ Attend a concert at the Grand Ole Opry
- ❐ Learn to play the piano
- ❐ Attend an Atlanta Braves home game*
- ❐ See a herd of Buffalo in the wild
- ❐ See a Black Bear in the wild
- ❐ Own a Mercedes Benz
- ❐ Eat lobster in Boston
- ❐ Snow ski in Aspen
- ❐ Own a cabin, overlooking a mountain lake

- ❐ Swim across the Mississippi
- ❐ Compete in the Iron Man
- ❐ Climb to the top of all of the highest mountains in the U.S.
- ❐ Raft the Colorado River
- ❐ Visit the Great Pyramids in Egypt
- ❐ Grow a garden each spring
- ❐ Host a conservative talk radio program
- ❐ Exercise for thirty minutes daily*
- ❐ Teach a class at a community college
- ❐ Observe a moose in the wild*
- ❐ Keep a daily journal
- ❐ Be a world renowned professional speaker
- ❐ Trace my family's history
- ❐ Earn a black belt in a martial art
- ❐ Be a witness for Christ each day
- ❐ "Escape" from Alcatraz by swimming off the island

 * These are goals I have reached.

DREAMS

"We grow great by dreams. All big men are dreamers. They see things in the soft haze of a spring day or in the red fire of a long winter's evening. Some of us let these great dreams die, but others nourish and protect them; nurse them through bad days till they bring them to the sunshine and light which comes always to those who sincerely hope that their dreams will come true."

—WOODROW WILSON

COUNT YOUR BLESSINGS

Soup's On!

Soup's On!

"We've become so spoiled in this country that we aren't even grateful for the things that were considered a miracle a hundred years ago."

—Jay "Patch" Platt

When I decided to thru-hike the Appalachian Trail, in all honesty, I had no idea of what to expect. I assumed it would be physically challenging and would take plenty of mental toughness to complete, and I certainly wasn't wrong in those assumptions.

What I didn't count on, however, was how many valuable lessons the trail would teach me—lessons I've discussed throughout this book.

Of the many lessons I learned on the trail, one stands out in my mind. It's a lesson I was taught during my first week as a thru-hiker, in the wilderness of Northern Maine; and it was reinforced throughout my hike. (I'll discuss this in more detail later.)

As I alluded to earlier, the beginning of my thru-hike found me naïve as to what it takes to complete such an endeavor.

I'd had plenty of field training as a Marine, having spent many days and nights in the wilderness all over the world, and I'd carried a heavy pack for many miles over the years. But I still had plenty to learn when it came to long distance hiking.

That fact became painfully obvious during my first week out, which was one of hardest of the entire hike, by far.

When I left for Maine to begin my hike, I didn't carry enough food with me—against the better advice of my wife.

Her recommendation was that I should take more than enough for the first week, or at least until I figured out my pace. I, being a hard head, didn't listen.

I knew that I had to go 120 miles to get to my first resupply point. This included crossing an area known as the "100 Mile Wilderness."

In my planning, I thought that I'd easily do twenty miles per day. At that pace, it would only take me six days to get to my resupply point.

As a buffer, I added a day to that estimate, to account for the unforeseen. So, even with the buffer day, I figured it would take me no more than seven days to get resupplied.

With that plan in mind, I began my hike with only seven days worth of food. The problem was, it took me nine full days to do the mileage. Why? There are several reasons, but blisters are at the top.

For some reason, I thought I was impervious to blisters and such. After all, I'd carried a pack for twenty or more miles many times as a Marine without getting a blister. But oh how wrong I was.

I'd bought a brand new pair of boots for the hike, and hadn't had time to properly break them in before my departure.

The new boots, combined with the odd angles my feet were placed in while going up and down the granite rock mountains of the north really did a number on my feet.

Those blisters I thought I'd never see began appearing within the first few miles of the first day.

To make matters worse, I didn't have anything (Moleskin, Band-Aids) to put on my feet once the blisters began.

Fortunately, I found some duct tape in a shelter on day three. I used it as a makeshift skin protector by wrapping it around my feet and over the blisters. Although painful, it did allow me to continue hiking.

With my feet in such poor shape, my plan for doing twenty-mile days now had a major bug in it.

At this point, I was only able to squeeze out 13-15 milers, and became aware of the inevitability that I was going to run out of food. So, I began to conserve every crumb.

By the eighth day, I was out of food. That day, I hiked for eight straight hours in a torrential downpour only to arrive at a shelter that was fully occupied. Some of the northbound hikers there told me of another shelter just a few miles south.

I still had a couple of hours of daylight left, and so decided to push on. This turned out to be a bad decision.

I didn't realize how much the rain had flooded the rivers and creeks. After crossing several of them, I was wetter and more tired than ever.

It had taken me over an hour to go less than two miles, and the sun was beginning to head west rapidly. So, I decided to stop and camp for the night by a river.

I wasn't carrying a tent at the time, just a tarp. The rain had tapered off a bit, and it was only lightly misting now. But the temperature was dropping quickly.

I began to shiver and knew I needed to get out of the wet stuff and into something dry. That's when I discovered that the rain had completely soaked my pack and its contents, including my sleeping bag and clothing.

"A man should always consider how much he has more than he wants, and how much more unhappy he might be than he really is."
—Joseph Addison

At this point, I felt like just sitting down and crying. Not only was I wet, tired and hungry; I was also seriously concerned about hypothermia.

After spending several minutes throwing a "pity party" for myself, I finally snapped out of it and began to work on rectifying the situation.

As a Marine, I'd gone through cold weather training several times over the years. So, I decided I'd put some of that training to good use.

The first thing I did was break out my wet sleeping bag. I squeezed out all the excess water I could and laid it out on the tarp. I then stripped out of my wet clothing and, with them in tow, got into the bag.

My training had taught me that my body heat would transfer to the bag, which, in turn, would warm me and dry my wet clothes.

So there I lay in my wet sleeping bag, with my wet clothes all around me—naked and shivering.

I waited there as the seconds became minutes, and the minutes turned to hours. After several hours, I decided that this method wasn't working. My gear was still soaked, and I was freezing.

I found my knit cap and placed it on my head and then got dressed in the driest gear I could find. I needed something to warm me up.

The rain had subsided a bit, so it seemed like the perfect time to prepare something to eat. After all, there's nothing like a hot meal to warm you up.

Unfortunately, I had no real food to speak of. I'd eaten my last bit that morning, so I decided it was time to get inventive. As I rifled through my supplies, I searched for anything which could be considered edible. There wasn't much. I had some green tea, sugar, salt and a bottle of Tabasco sauce. "Sounds like the makings of soup," I mused.

I combined all three tea bags, a cup of boiling water, a tablespoon of salt, and two tablespoons of the Tabasco sauce. While not the best soup I've ever had, it did sustain me. It provided much more than nutritive value, though. It taught me a valuable lesson that we all need to remember.

The lesson? Simply this: Be grateful for all that you have. Even though the soup I had wasn't much in the way of meal, it was more than some starving children had that night. And that soup, as meager as it was, reminded me of just how blessed I am—and that we all are.

The problem is, most of us take so much for granted—particularly as Americans. We often forget that it's only by the grace of God that we even live in such a country as we do. A country whose citizens enjoy the freedoms we share—freedoms which shouldn't be taken lightly, freedoms so wonderful that men and women have died to preserve them.

The freedom of speech and press and having the freedom to worship the God of your choice, or none at all, are just a few of the privileges that we enjoy, and that many in the world do not.

As wonderful as those freedoms are, there are many others that we don't even consciously think about.

We've become so spoiled in this country that we aren't even grateful for the things that were considered a miracle a hundred years ago.

For instance, when we turn on a light switch, we just expect a light to come on. We also expect to have hot water for a bath, and we expect to get three hot meals a day. We expect, we expect, we expect.

How about you? Are you grateful? Do you realize how truly blessed you are? Or do you grumble your way through life, complaining about this or that?

I've actually heard people say that nothing is good in their life, or that they have nothing to be thankful for. That's really sad.

These people have the audacity to say this as they are standing on two strong, healthy legs. I'll bet someone in a wheelchair would be grateful for those legs.

Or, as they look out of two perfect eyes. I'm sure a blind person would be grateful for those eyes.

Or, how about the person who, after spending an hour stuffing their face at an all-you-can-eat buffet, does nothing but complain about how tough their steak was? I'm sure that homeless child who went without supper last night would gladly take that steak.

I could go on and on, but I think you get the idea. If only we'd spend more time looking for what's right in our life, instead of always looking for what's wrong, we'd find there's plenty to be thankful for.

I'll end this chapter with a portion of a poem by an unknown author that I believe sums up the chapter's essence. "I once was distraught because I had no shoes, until I met a man who had no feet." That really says it all. So be grateful for all that you have, even if it is just soup!

I AM BLESSED INDEED

Today upon a bus, I saw a lovely girl, I envied her: She seemed so happy. And I wish I were as fair. And then, suddenly, she rose to leave, and I saw her hobble down the aisle, She had one leg and wore a crutch, But as she passed, she smiled.

Oh God, forgive me when I whine, I have two legs, I am blessed indeed. The world is mine!

Later, walking down the street, I saw a man with eyes of blue. But he just stood and watched the others play. So, I stopped a moment and then I said, "Why don't you join the others, sir?" But he looked ahead without a word. And then I knew he could not hear.

Oh God, forgive me when I whine, I have two ears, I am blessed indeed. The world is mine!

And later, I stopped to buy some sweets. The lad who sold them had such charm, I talked with him. If I were late, it would do no harm. But as I turned to go, he said to me, "I thank you sir. You've been so kind. It's nice to talk with folks like you." "You see," he said, "I am blind."

Oh God, forgive me when I whine, I have two eyes, I am blessed indeed. The world is mine!

With legs to take me where I want to go, With ears to hear the things I need to know, With eyes to watch that radiant sunset glow.

Oh God, forgive me when I whine, I am blessed indeed! The world is mine!

—OG MANDINO

Lesson Ten

Free Yourself

Check Your Pack

CHECK YOUR PACK

*"...by lightening your load, and
only carrying the important stuff,
your life can change for the
better."*

—JAY "PATCH" PLATT

What's your pack weigh? It's one of the most common questions asked on the AT. As a hiker, pack weight can be an important indicator of many things. How far and fast you can go for instance.

The idea is to carry as little as possible, and still be able to survive in relative comfort. In other words, you only carry the necessities, with a few "luxury" items thrown in for good measure. The last thing you want to do is carry unnecessary weight. As a thru-hiker, I had a lot to learn in this area.

When I was a Marine, pack weight was never that much of an issue. Our packs were heavy—loaded with rations, ammunition, extra gear, etc. Added to that was the weight of whatever weapon you were carrying at the time.

Although their packs were heavy, most Marines wouldn't dare complain that they were too much for them to carry; that would be a sign of weakness.

On the contrary, most Marines consider the ability to carry a heavy pack a sign of strength and ruggedness.

You may not agree with that philosophy, but it's a part of the competitive nature of being a Marine.

So that's the kind of thinking that had been ingrained in me for over fourteen years, and that's the logic I carried to the trail.

Proudly, I left for Maine with my pack weighing over seventy-five pounds. In it I had stuffed everything that I could possibly think of that I might need during my hike.

Fortunately, I met some great people along the way who helped me fix my thinking. In the process I learned that much of what I was carrying was excess baggage, or simply unnecessary.

Heavy books, a metal shovel, and bulky clothing are just a few examples.

Over the months, as I learned to whittle down my pack weight, I noticed the trail got less and less difficult—but it was never easy.

What I learned about pack weight and the importance of only carrying useful stuff in one's pack, turned out to be quite a valuable lesson—one that I believe applies to all of us in our everyday lives.

Now, you may be wondering what in the world carrying a pack has to do with you. But, if you go back to the metaphor of "hiking the trail of life" that we discuss throughout this book, you'll see how it applies.

By checking the "pack" that you're carrying on your "hike" and then eliminating what you don't need, your whole life can change for the better.

It's amazing how much useless junk most of us carry around on a daily basis. Our "packs" are full of it. Let me give you some examples of what to look for in yours.

Living in the past. Are you allowing yourself to be bogged down by past experiences? Do you constantly daydream about days gone by? "Living in the past" keeps you from moving ahead and adds a tremendous amount of weight to your "pack."

Both good and bad memories have the ability to hold you back by causing you to dwell on them, instead of creating new ones.

For instance, maybe you were hurt by someone long ago and can't seem to get over it. Or maybe you still have feelings for someone, even though they've made it clear they no longer have those same feelings for you.

These types of emotional hurts are all too common. Believe me, I've been there, too. But what I've learned is, you can't grow until you let them go. Holding on to those feelings will just eat you up inside. It's like picking at a scab. The wound will never heal until you leave it alone. Although there may be a scar that remains, if you do allow the healing process to take place, it will eventually heal.

You may be thinking, "That sounds great, but how do I go about doing it?" It's actually a simple process, though not necessarily easy.

You don't have to do some of the things I've done in the past to help myself get over painful memories.

I've gone as far as picturing the person in question while smelling a jar full of rotten eggs, causing myself to get sick to my stomach. I've also popped myself with a rubber band each time I thought of the person.

These methods work, by the way, but they aren't very pleasant.

You could also spend hundreds, or thousands, of dollars on a head shrink, with no guarantee that you'll ever get any results.

Or you could do what I'm recommending here. It doesn't require anything special and can be done in seconds.

First, you've got to be sure that you're really ready to move on. This method won't work if you don't commit to it.

"You can't have a better tomorrow
if you are thinking about
yesterday all the time."

—CHARLES F. KETTERING

Once you've made a firm decision to move on, picture the person in question, as if they were there with you. Then, stating their name, simply say the words "I forgive you" (e.g., "Joe Smucatelli, I forgive you").

That's it. That's all it takes. Once you've forgiven them, get on with your life. You don't have to make a big production out of it. And you don't need to call the person up to tell them what you've done, or to let them know that you're now getting on with your life.

Actually, it really doesn't matter whether they know or not anyway because you're not forgiving them so much for their sake as for yours.

They might not even realize that they've hurt you so badly. Chances are, they've moved on with their life. Meanwhile, you've still been holding on to all of the anger, sadness, regret, etc. It's time to move on.

Another way many people "live in the past" and thus are held back is by holding on to memories of their "glory" years. They sit around and think about how great things used to be. Meanwhile, their life is crumbling around them.

I know some guys who have fallen into this trap. They constantly talk about the "big game" in high school and how great an athlete they were. But they couldn't run around the block now; they drink a six-pack a day and smoke like a chimney. They're living in the land of used-to-be's, and as motivational speaker Les Brown says, "Used-to-be's don't make no honey."

So, the key in dealing with the past is this: Respect it for what it is, HISTORY. Learn from it, admire it, do whatever you need to with it, but don't live in it.

Worry and anxiety. Do you find yourself worrying about all the things that might happen or could go wrong in your life? Are you anxious about the future, wondering what it will hold for you? If so, then you've got another couple of big items to remove from your pack.

Worry and anxiety do you no good whatsoever. What you have to understand is   that there are some things you can control and some you cannot. The key is knowing the difference.

For instance, you cannot control the future. What happens, happens. You can plan and hope all you want and I'm certainly not saying you shouldn't. but it should be done with the realization that your future is not promised.

I'm sure most of us hope to be around for a hundred healthy years or more. Still, there is no guarantee that we will even see tomorrow.

The bottom line is this: If you're spending a whole lot of time dwelling on what the future might hold, you're simply holding yourself back from living fully in the present.

"The greatest discovery of my generation is that human beings can alter their lives by altering their attitudes of mind."

—WILLIAM JAMES

Just as you can't control the future, you also can't control all the "might's" in your life. Your spouse might leave you, you might get cancer, you might get fired from your job, you might...

While it's true that all those things might happen, just as easily, they might not. The question is, why bother worrying about it when you have absolutely no control over what might happen?

All you can do, is be the best spouse possible and not give your mate a reason to leave, eat right, exercise, be the most productive employee at your job, etc. Then, if something does happen in your life, handle it.

So the key in dealing with worry and anxiety is remembering to keep them in perspective. Understand the things you can and cannot change, and then deal with life as it happens.

Self. How do you see yourself? This is an important question to answer. You can be your best friend or your worst enemy. Your biggest fan, or worst critic. You can talk yourself up or beat yourself down. It's your choice.

It's unfortunate how many people don't understand this. That's part of the reason why so many people have such a lack of self-confidence and a poor self-image.

Understanding this gives you the opportunity to determine how you choose to look at yourself, what you say to yourself, etc.

By far, the most effective way to positively influence yourself is through self-talk. You control what you say to yourself—good, bad, or indifferent. Therefore, make sure what you say counts.

Another highly effective method to improve your sense of self is to, "Act as if." This simply means that you act as if you already have the qualities that you want to possess, before you actually possess them. If you "act as if" long enough, in time, you will actually possess those qualities.

People. Finally, let me suggest that you take a close look at the people around you. They too may be excess weight that you're carrying around, which serves no valuable purpose.

The kind of people I'm referring to here are easy to spot, because they actually make you feel worse after being around them a short while. They're negative, cynical, critical and generally unhappy with their own lives, and so they want to bring others down with them.

For your own sake, you need to limit your time around them, because they're just no good for you. (Of course, if you're married to them, seek counseling.)

One final note here is, if you see yourself as the kind of negative person I've just described, it's never too late to change. But, the time to do it is now—before someone drops you from their pack.

These are but a few of the items you could be carrying that are weighing you down. It's up to you to search through your own pack, and see what's in it. No one can really do that but you.

I assure you that by lightening your load and only carrying what's important, your life can change for the better. So, get up and go check your pack.

TRUE FREEDOM

"To laugh is to risk appearing the fool. To weep is to risk being called sentimental. To reach out to another is to risk involvement. To expose feelings is to risk showing your true self. To place your ideas and your dreams before a crowd is to risk being called naive. To love is to risk not being loved in return. To live is to risk dying. To hope is to risk despair, and to try is to risk failure. But risks must be taken, because the greatest risk in life is to risk nothing. The person, who risks nothing, does nothing, has nothing, is nothing, and becomes nothing. He may avoid suffering and sorrow, but he simply cannot learn and feel and change and grow and love and live. Chained by things that are certain, he is a slave. He has forfeited his freedom. Only the person who risks is truly free."

—UNKNOWN

APPENDIX

"WHAT IS VHL?"

Von Hippel-Lindau, or VHL, is a genetic condition involving the abnormal growth of blood vessels in some parts of the body which are particularly rich in blood vessels.

While blood vessels normally grow like trees, in people with VHL, little knots of capillaries sometimes occur. These little knots are called angiomas, or hemangioblastomas. These angiomas may cause problems themselves, or problems can develop around them.

Dr. Eugen von Hippel described the angiomas in the eye in 1904. His name is usually associated with VHL in the retina, though even in his original case study, his patients had tumors in places other than the eye.

Dr. Arvid Lindau described the angiomas of the cerebellum and spine in 1926. His name is usually associated with occurrences of VHL in the central nervous system.

Types of Angiomas: The angioma may occur in a delicate place where the pressure it exerts may cause symptoms. Angiomas in the brain or spinal cord, for example, may press on nerve or brain tissue and cause symptoms, such as headaches.

As the angioma grows, the walls of the blood vessels may weaken and some blood leakage may occur, causing damage to surrounding tissues. Blood leakage from angiomas in the retina, for instance, can interfere with vision.

Cysts may also form around the angiomas. Cysts are fluid-filled sacs which may exert pressure or create blockages which can cause symptoms.

Cysts and tumors can occur in the kidney, pancreas, liver, or adrenal glands, as well as the eyes, brain and spinal cord. Some of these tumors are benign, while others are cancerous.

How Do People get VHL? Von Hippel-Lindau is a genetically transmitted condition. It is caused by a dominant gene. Even in people who have this gene, however, there is a wide variation in the date of onset of the disease, the organ system in which the problem occurs, and the severity of the involvement. Every person is different.

VHL occurs in every ethnic group, everywhere in the world. Overall, it's estimated that about one person in 32,000 has VHL, worldwide.

The VHL Family Alliance: The VHL Family Alliance is a voluntary, non-profit group dedicated to improving the diagnosis, treatment, and quality of life of individuals and families affected by Von Hippel-Lindau disease.

If you'd like further information on VHL, or would like to donate to the VHL Family Alliance, you can reach them by phone at 1-800-767-4VHL, by email at info@vhl.org, or you can visit them on the web at www.vhl.org.

THE END OF THE TRAIL

Well, we've reached the end of the trail together. We certainly covered a lot of terrain along the way. I hope you learned a thing or two that you can put to good use in your own life. Now, I need to ask a favor of you.

I have a powerful desire to share the lessons in this book with as many people as possible, and I know there is nothing more effective than a strong recommendation from a "satisfied customer."

While I am obviously interested in selling more books, my primary motive is to help others. You can help me accomplish that by your willingness to spread the word about *A Time to Walk: Life Lessons Learned on the Appalachian Trail*.

In doing so, you just might provide someone with what they need, to show them that their life is worth living after all.

Finally, as we go our separate ways, keep this in mind. Where one trail ends, another begins. Your "hike" goes on for a lifetime. So follow your path and keep moving forward, and I'll see you on top of the mountain.

HAPPY TRAILS,
JAY "PATCH" PLATT

ABOUT THE AUTHOR

Jay "Patch" Platt, a retired Marine Corps Gunnery Sergeant, is one of fewer than three hundred people ever to have completed a south-bound thru-hike of the Appalachian Trail.

Jay is a popular speaker, seminar leader and writer in the areas of human motivation and potential. He delivers his uplifting presentations to businesses, associations, and educational institutions throughout the country.

Jay resides in Cartersville, Georgia, with his wife, Paz, and their two dogs, Jake and Sadie.

If you'd like further information on any of Jay's books, tapes, or speaking presentations, visit him on the web at www.jayplatt.com, or call him toll free at (888) 404-6598.